YOU SUCK, SIR

CHRONICLES OF A HIGH SCHOOL ENGLISH TEACHER AND THE SMARTASS STUDENTS WHO SCHOOLED HIM

PAUL BAE

ROBIN'S EGG BOOKS
AN IMPRINT OF
ARSENAL PULP PRESS
VANCOUVER

ROBIN'S EGG BOOKS is an imprint of
ARSENAL PULP PRESS
Suite 202 – 211 East Georgia St.
Vancouver, BC V6A 1Z6
Canada
arsenalpulp.com

The publisher gratefully acknowledges the support of the Canada Council for the Arts and the British Columbia Arts Council for its publishing program, and the Government of Canada, and the Government of British Columbia (through the Book Publishing Tax Credit Program), for its publishing activities.

Arsenal Pulp Press acknowledges the xʷməθkʷəy̓əm (Musqueam), Sḵwx̱wú7mesh (Squamish), and səl̓ilwətaʔɬ (Tsleil-Waututh) Nations, custodians of the traditional, ancestral, and unceded territories where our office is located. We pay respect to their histories, traditions, and continuous living cultures and commit to accountability, respectful relations, and friendship.

Front cover design by Oliver McPartlin
Back cover and text design by Jazmin Welch
Edited by Charles Demers
Copy edited by Shirarose Wilensky
Proofread by Alison Strobel

Printed and bound in Canada

Library and Archives Canada Cataloguing in Publication:
Title: You suck, sir : chronicles of a high school English teacher and the smartass students who schooled him / Paul Bae.
Names: Bae, Paul, author.
Identifiers: Canadiana (print) 20190231106 | Canadiana (ebook) 20190231165 | ISBN 9781551528076 (softcover) | ISBN 9781551528083 (HTML)
Subjects: LCSH: Bae, Paul. | LCSH: High school teachers—British Columbia—Vancouver—Anecdotes. | LCSH: High school students—British Columbia—Vancouver—Anecdotes. | LCSH: Teacher-student relationships—British Columbia—Vancouver—Anecdotes. | LCSH: High school teaching—British Columbia—Vancouver—Anecdotes.
Classification: LCC LA2325.B34 A3 2020 | DDC 371.10092—dc23

YOU SUCK, SIR

This book is dedicated to the three public school
teachers who changed my life: Glen Lapthorne,
who first brought me out of my shell; Marlena Morgan,
who helped me find my voice; and Anand Atal,
who prepared me for the wider world.

And to the most inspiring people I've ever known:
my students.

ACKNOWLEDGMENTS

This book grew out of my eponymously named blog, which ran from 2012 to 2015, and contains some of the original posts. (More on that in the afterword.)

Thank you to my friend and editor Charles Demers for not only choosing *You Suck, Sir* for his Arsenal Pulp Press imprint Robin's Egg Books but also helping me give it shape.

And thank you to my wife, Lani, for her ceaseless patience and support when I had nowhere else to find what I needed to give to these young people.

FOREWORD

I am an older brother, the product of a marriage between an oldest brother and an oldest sister (Jesus, *of course* from separate families— how could you even ask a thing like that?!). I am an oldest cousin to a brood of Anglo-Scotch Western Canadians, as well as to a *broude* of Québécois *cousins et cousines*. In other words, I have never experienced the intimate pedagogical cruelty and guidance offered by the best of older brothers—the loving combination of one hand extended to help hold you steady on the journey into maturity, while the other is slipping behind your back to tack on a *Kick Me* sign. At least, I never had that until I met Paul Bae. (I have argued on several occasions that having a Korean older brother should theoretically serve to mitigate my white privilege but have been empathically told: "No dice.")

In 2005, five years into his comedy career and one into mine, Paul introduced himself to me and invited me to form, with him, a sketch comedy duo. Drawing on a piece of appropriated Buddhist wisdom (or at least re-appropriated in the aftermath of the evangelization of the southern tip of the Korean Peninsula—and usually missionaries are so judgmental about southern tips!) to the effect that only that which is empty can be filled, Paul dubbed us "Bucket," and we quickly marketed ourselves as Vancouver's first and only biracial, bi-sizal comedy duo.

Identifying each other as members of the same exclusive tribe— that of intellectual snobs with nevertheless low-brow sensibilities—we gigglingly put together sketches in which no highfalutin subjects were off limits for being either too cerebral or too juvenile: a man who goes to his doctor after an episode of unprotected sex sends his balls rolling pointlessly from side to side ("You have Sisyphus."); two murder detectives dance with plungers in a musical number about Derrida in *CSI: Pretentious Victims Unit*; the devil on somebody's shoulder turns up for a shift, only to find that his counterpart has ditched the wings and halo for a T-shirt that says *Super Ego*, and wants him to wear one that says *Id*. I forget how exactly we discovered that my favourite and most influential high school teacher, Marlena Morgan, had been Paul's mentor during his student-teacher practicum—but I do remember that even though we were thrilled with surprise, we weren't shocked. She had left us both with the same love and excitement, and irreverence, for big ideas.

Paul has a resumé more eclectic than a Depression-era carny (and is, in my experience, just as trustworthy), but a clear thread connects everything he's ever done, from the youth pastor's pulpit to the stand-up comedy stage to the classroom: he teaches, through story. Today, he's doing that on a larger scale—teaching the cast and crew of a Marvel superhero podcast, for instance, that it actually isn't funny to ask Method Man if he's a method actor (even though it kind of is)—but he's the same guy.

I'm honoured to be Paul Bae's pale little brother, and to present this hilarious and compelling collection of his teaching stories. From Sir, with love.

CHARLES DEMERS
Robin's Egg Books Editor

FUNNY GUY

A grade ten student is laughing hysterically at a joke I made in class. I've been waiting for about a minute for her to stop so I can continue the lesson.

HER (Between gasps of breath) "I'm ... sorry! So ... funny."

ME "Please, don't apologize. You make me feel like the funniest person alive."

HER "I know! I laugh ... at the stupidest ... things!"

I am at a week-long grade eight orientation camp. It's after lights out and everyone is in their rooms. My room is next to a group of grade eight boys and the walls are so thin I can hear everything they say.

STUDENT 1 "Wait. Do you think Sir can hear us?"

Silence.

STUDENT 2 (Calling out) "Sir?"

Silence.

STUDENT 2 (Yelling) "Sir! Can you hear us?"

Silence.

STUDENT 2 "No, he can't hear us."

For the remainder of the week, these boys think I'm psychic.

ANOTHER SUMMER COME AND GONE

ME "What did you do this summer?"
GRADE TEN STUDENT "Nothing much. Hung out at the mall a lot."
ME "You know when Benja—"
HER "Are you going to bring up the Benjamin Franklin story?"
ME "How'd you know?"
HER "Everyone knows."
ME "Well, he *did* start his own newspaper when he was your age."

HER "Are you actually comparing me to one of the greatest men in American history? That's the standard I have to live up to? Were you doing that at his age?"

ME "Good point."

TOO YOUNG TO RECALL 9/11

STUDENT 1 "Why's everyone saying 'never forget'?"
STUDENT 2 "You know: never forget. Like, don't forget it."
STUDENT 1 "Don't forget what?"
STUDENT 2 "I don't know. Something."

GULLIBLE

One of my English 8 students excitedly approaches my desk, his buddies in tow, all giggling.

HIM "Sir, do you know someone wrote *gullible* on your shoes?"
ME "Really?"
HIM "Yeah, look!"
ME "That's so weird, cuz someone spray-painted *sucker* on the ceiling today."

He looks up. His friends start howling with laughter. It takes him a few seconds to realize what just happened, and then he looks at me in hurt disbelief.

I put a hand on his shoulder.

ME "Trust me, kid, you wouldn't respect me if I had looked down."

PERFUME

ME "Sonia, do you mind not wearing that perfume to class anymore? I'm allergic to it."

HER "How?"

ME "I get a runny nose and my eyes are itchy."

HER "Hey, the exact same thing happens to me!"

GENERATION GAP

Sometimes I'm reminded of the huge generation gap between my students and me.

The other day, for a laugh, as I dramatically entered the classroom a minute after the bell rang, I yelled, "Who let the dogs out?"

Half the class looked out the window. For dogs.

THE DUDE

During grade twelve English class ...

STUDENT "Dude, I don't get this."

ME "Don't call me *dude*."

STUDENT "Sir?"

ME "Yes."

STUDENT "But you're more like a dude, not a *sir*."

HIS BUDDY "Yeah, sir. You're, like, *the dude*."

ME (Bashfully) "Well, just for today, then. *Dude* it is."

MOISTURIZER

GRADE TEN STUDENT "Sir, do you have any moisturizer? My hands are really dry."

ME "Sorry. Don't have any."

HER "Really? You don't have any at all? Even a little bit?"

ME "Trust me, I'm not holding back any moisturizer."

HER "You never know."

SHOWERS

GRADE EIGHT STUDENT "Sir, the gym teacher makes us take showers after class."

ME "Yeah, that's the system here. It's hygienic."

HIM "But it's all of us in one big shower room with our junk hanging out in front of everyone. It's creepy."

ME "You'll get used to it."

HIM "That's creepier!"

BREAKING UP IS HARD TO DO ... USUALLY

GRADE TEN STUDENT "Sir, do you regret breaking up with any of your girlfriends?"

ME "No, because all that experience allowed me to mature to get the amazing girlfriend I have now."

HER "So, guys don't regret breakups?"

ME "Sure they do, at the time. But we all move on."

It's not the answer she was looking for.

ME (As sympathetically as possible) "You know, I'm sure that there's at least a small part of him that will regret leaving you."

HER (Shocked, then laughing) "Leaving *me*? Oh, hell no! I left him. I just want to make sure I didn't hurt him too bad."

ME "Give him a few days."

GOOD CROWD

GRADE ELEVEN STUDENT "Sir, I don't have you for English this year."

ME "I noticed that. Too bad."

HIM "This sucks."

ME "If it's any consolation, I repeat my jokes every year, so it'd be kind of boring for you."

HIM "I'd still laugh. Half of your jokes weren't even that funny, but I laughed anyways."

ME "I guess you're really polite."

HIM "Yeah, probably."

FU

ME "What did you just say to that student?"

GRADE NINE STUDENT "Nothing."

ME "Tell me what you said."

HIM "I told him FU."

ME "You know that's unacceptable."

HIM "It's not swearing. It's just letters."

ME "All swearing is just letters."

PROTECTION

NEW GRADE NINE STUDENT "Are there bullies here?"

ME "There are bullies everywhere. But our school has a strict anti-bullying policy. If you feel threatened by anyone, you come see me and I'll take care of it."

HIM "You'll beat them up for me?"

ME "No."

HIM "Then what good are you?"

THE SUB

I have just returned from a three-day absence.

GRADE TWELVE STUDENT "Sir, can you get that substitute teacher in for you next time you're sick?"

ME "He was that good?"

HER "He was so dreamy!"

The rest of the girls in the class nod enthusiastically.

ME "What did the guys think?"

GRADE TWELVE BOY "I guess he was pretty good-looking."

ME "I mean his teaching."

HIM "Oh. It was all right."

(Note: Years later, this substitute teacher would become Canada's prime minister. Yes, it was Justin Trudeau.)

IPHONE DETAILS

I have instructed the grade eight students to use their senses to write a descriptive paragraph about their favourite possession.

STUDENT "Sir, how's this?"

ME "It's good. But why do you describe what your iPhone tastes like?"

HIM "Because I accidentally licked it once."

ME "Accidentally?"

HIM "You don't want to go there."

SMORGASBORD

GRADE EIGHT STUDENT "Sir, your lunch smells really good."

ME "Thanks. Made it myself."

HIM "Wow. Is that Korean?"

ME "This ... lasagna?"

HIM "Yeah."

ME "No."

HIM "I didn't think so."

FRACTIONS

I am covering another teacher's Math 9 class, on the subject of fractions.

ME "Okay, John and Ed are roommates and they've just ordered a pizza. There are eight slices. Now, John starts eating and leaves Ed three slices. How much of the pizza did John eat?"

STUDENT "A douche amount."

ORIENTAL

GRADE TWELVE STUDENT "Sir, is 'Oriental' a bad word?"

ME "No."

HIM "But it's considered offensive?"

ME "To Asians, yes."

HIM "But how about 'Oriental rug'? Is that offensive?"

ME "I don't think the rug will be offended."

HIM "Oh. Okay."

ME "Really? That's it? You're not going to challenge me on that?"

HIM "I just want to be careful not to offend you cuz you're Oriental."

BREAKFAST OF CHAMPIONS

It's before the first bell and I'm in my classroom eating an Egg McMuffin and hash brown with my coffee. One of my grade ten students walks in early.

HER "Sir, you call that breakfast?"

ME "Yes, I do."

HER "Do you know what's in that sandwich?"

ME "Yes. But I was in a rush and didn't have time to make my breakfast."

HER "Being in a rush is no excuse. Can you imagine all the factory farms and pollutants that could be reduced if people like you stopped being in a rush?"

ME "Are you trying to guilt me out of this breakfast?"

HER "Yeah. Is it working?"

ME "Totally."

HER "My work here is done."

SPACE INVADER

GRADE TEN STUDENT "Sir, what's the first video game you ever played?"

ME "In an arcade? Probably *Space Invaders*."

HIM "Was it like *Halo*?"

ME "Nothing like it. It was just a block of spaceships and you had to shoot them down while hiding behind a bunch of houses."

HIM "That's it?"

ME "They sped up a bit each stage."

HIM "No wonder your generation read more books than us."

VIDEO GAME DROPOUT

A grade ten student has told me he is considering dropping out of school ...

HIM "Sir, don't bother trying to talk me out of it. It's my decision."

ME "I'm worried about what you're going to do for a living."

HIM "I told you: I want to be a professional gamer."

ME "Are you any good?"

HIM "Yeah. Real good."

ME "I mean, are you ranked in the top five, ten or twenty in the country?"

HIM "Not yet."

ME "Then why drop out now? Why not wait until you're making money from it?"

HIM "Cuz school's wasting my time."

ME "So, to avoid wasting your time, you play video games?"

HIM "Well, it sounds silly the way you say it."

(He did not drop out.)

A LETTER WILL DO

A grade ten student brings her marked essay up to me.

HER "Sir, why'd you circle that?"

ME "That's an *R*."

HER "So?"

ME "We spell it A-R-E."

HER "But why use a bunch of letters when one will do?"

ME "You're right. How's the letter *F*?"

HER "I'll make the corrections."

MAGIC

GRADE TWELVE STUDENT "Sir, did you go to your prom?"

ME "Yes."

HIM "Was it fun?"

ME "It was magical."

HIS BUDDY "That means he got lucky that night."

ME "No. That means you and I go to different types of magic shows."

SWEET REWARD

One of my popular, athletic English 9 students strolls into class with a small entourage in tow, a beaming smile on his face. He hands me a chocolate bar.

HIM "Yo, sir, it's for you."

ME "Thanks. What's the occasion?"

HIM "The vending machine spit out an extra one when I bought this one."

He's holding another bar.

ME "Why don't you give it to one of your crew here?"
HIM "They don't deserve it."

They all look sheepishly at their shoes as if in shameful agreement.

ME "Well, that's not entirely true. Michael here made that attempt
to help you out last week, as misguided as it was."
HIM "When?"
ME "Remember I caught you cheating on that test? Michael almost
showed you his answers until I caught you."
HIM "Oh yeah! I forgot."

He gives Michael the chocolate bar.

A POEM FOR HER

GRADE ELEVEN STUDENT "Sir, have you ever written a poem
for a girl?"
ME "Yes. I was about your age."
HIM "How did she take it?"
ME "She wasn't impressed."
HIM "I thought girls liked that kind of stuff."
ME "Here's the thing: if a girl already likes you, she'll find it
romantic. If she's on the fence about you, she'll find it creepy."
HIM "Really?"
ME "I don't know. That's how I justified it in my mind."

STRANGE MAGIC

A couple of my grade eight students are laughing behind my back while I'm at the board.

ME "What's up, gentlemen?"

They start giggling like madmen.

ME "Spit it out. I won't be offended."
STUDENT "You've got a wedgie, sir."

The other students start laughing.

ME "Well, what would be the least embarrassing way of dealing with it? Should I do the popular walk and shake?"

I saunter in front of the students swaying my hips. They are laughing.

ME "Or should I do the drop and squat?"

I drop my whiteboard marker and slowly squat to pick it up. The students are beside themselves. With a flourish, I get up and turn my back to the class.

STUDENT "You're like a magician!"

ADORABLE THEORY

GRADE EIGHT STUDENT "Sir, is there any way to open these windows wider?"
ME "No, that's as wide as they go."
HER "Why do they design it this way?"
ME "They don't want anyone sneaking into the school through the windows."

HER "Or maybe it's a way to keep students in!"

ME "How's that?"

HER "Maybe it's so that students don't try to commit suicide by jumping out the windows."

ME "We're on the ground floor."

HER "You can still break your neck if you're tiny."

GOLF

GRADE TEN STUDENT "Sir, do you play golf?"

ME "No."

HIM "Why not?"

ME "Just never got into it."

HIM "Your father never wanted you to play golf?"

ME "Why the sudden interest in golf?"

HIM "I just want to know."

ME "Are you asking because I'm Korean?"

He hesitates.

ME "Well?"

HIM "Yeah."

ME "I knew it. Stereotyper!"

Some students laugh.

HIM "So, did your dad try to make you golf?"

FLATTERY

GRADE TWELVE STUDENT "Sir, nice shirt!"

ME "Thanks."

HIM "You have a keen eye for fashion."

ME "Well, my girlfriend got it for me."

HIM "Then you have great taste in women."

ME "Do you need an extension on your homework?"

HIM "And a mind reader, too!"

ME "Yes."

BRIGHT

In the middle of a lesson, a grade eleven student raises her hand.

ME "Yes?"

HER "Sir, can you close the curtains?"

ME "Why?"

HER "It's too bright."

ME "What are you? A vampire?"

HER "What do you have against vampires?"

ME "I wish I was that cool when I was your age."

FAME

One of my colleagues has invited me to make an appearance
in her class because a few of her English 10 students saw me on
a television program and had no idea I taught in the school. I give
a funny five-minute spiel to get the students laughing and then
take questions.

ME "Yes, you at the back?"

STUDENT "Why are you teaching? Why not do your comedy thing full time?"

ME "The simple answer is I love teaching. I quit teaching in 2002 to do comedy full time, and around 2009, I realized I was missing something, and that something was teaching."

HER "But don't you want to be famous?"

ME "I'm at an age where I only do things that make me happy or will add joy to my life. Teaching and comedy and writing make me happy. I personally don't know a single person who is made happy by being famous."

HER "You don't know enough famous people, then."

GETTING THE BOOT

GRADE ELEVEN STUDENT "Sir, what was your first job?"

ME "I got a warehouse job at a popular hiking boot company when I was in the grade ten."

HIM "Was the pay good?"

ME "Not really. But it was a family friend who hired me, and I did it so that I could get a discount on boots."

HIM "What kind of boots?"

ME "They were one of the first companies to make Gore-Tex boots, and I wanted a pair of them to impress the ladies."

HIM "You're telling me you took a warehouse job to save up for Gore-Tex boots to attract girls?"

ME "Yes."

HIM "Man, you had, like, no game at all."

JUST ONE LOOK

One of my grade nine students tells me that he thinks one of his classmates is attracted to him.

ME "What makes you think that?"

HIM "I keep catching her looking at me."

ME "Why are you looking at her?"

HIM "I don't know."

ME "So maybe she keeps looking at you because you keep looking at her."

HIM "You think?"

ME "I don't know. I'm asking you. Who's looking at whom?"

HIM "I don't know anymore."

OCTOBER

TAKING THE BULLET

There's a commotion at the back of the English 8 class.

ME "What's going on here?"

Two boys are making a huge fuss and leaning away in disgust from the shy new girl, who looks mortified.

BOY 1 "She farted, sir! It stinks."
ME "Sorry, fellas. That was me. I was hoping no one would notice. My bad."

I walk away. The class explodes in laughter at me. I glance at the new girl, who looks confused now.

You always hear stories of teachers sacrificing everything for their students. I now know that at the very least, for these kids, I'll take the blame for a fart.

BULLIES

Two of my students in grade ten were caught locking two smaller students in a closet. I have a chat with them.

ME "Do you know what a bully looks like?"

Both of them are deep in thought, drowning in their own shame. Then, Bully 1 slowly points at Bully 2. I stare at Bully 2. His eyes are averted.

ME (To Bully 2) "Do you know what a coward looks like?"

Bully 2 slowly points at Bully 1.

ESTIMATE

STUDENT "How old are you, sir? Thirty-five? Forty-eight?"

ME "How tall are you? Five eight? Six two?"

DISCOURSE

After a frustrating round of discussions with the English 9 class.

ME "I sometimes question the level of discourse."

STUDENT "Grade nine."

ME "What?"

HER "This course is grade nine."

ME "*DIS-course!*"

HER (Louder, and more slowly) "That's what I said!"

CELLPHONES

STUDENT "Sir, what kind of cellphone did you have growing up?"

ME "We didn't have any back then."

STUDENT "So you emailed a lot?"

ME "No one had computers yet."

STUDENT "So how'd you talk to girls?"

ME "With my mouth. You know, like we're doing right now."

HAVING CHILDREN

STUDENT "Do you have kids, sir?"

ME "No."

HIM "You gonna have kids one day?"

ME "No."

HIM "Why not?"

ME "I don't like kids."

HIM "Why not?"

ME "They ask too many personal questions."

HIM "They do?"

I look at him.

HIM "Oh."

After a moment.

HIM "You're talking about me, right?"

ME "Yes."

HIM "Got it."

KARMIC JUNGLE

I have a grade twelve student whom I've talked to on several occasions about thinking before she interrupts the class. Then, last week, on the topic of imports and exports ...

ME "You may have noticed that we import a lot of our products from Asia—"

HER "Asia, sir? Don't you mean China?"

ME (Trying to give her an out) "Well, yes, a lot of them are from China."

HER (Very smugly, to the class) "See? China. Not Asia."

And that's how students learn the hard way that karma sometimes sounds like a classroom full of laughter.

GHOSTS

STUDENT "Sir, do you believe in ghosts?"

ME "No."

HIM "Why not?"

ME "Because if ghosts exist, then science can't be trusted. Anything would go. Dragons, unicorns—"

ANOTHER STUDENT "Crocodiles."

ME "Yes. What?"

STOP, FIEF!

During the Middle Ages unit ...

GRADE NINE STUDENT "Sir, what's a fief?"

ME "It's what a guy with a speech impediment calls the guy who stole his wallet."

Silence in the class. Finally, one guy laughs. I point him out.

ME "See? Daryl got it."

DARYL (Barely able to speak from laughter) "No. I'm laughing at how bad the joke was."

NOT THIS TIME

GRADE TEN STUDENT "Sir, may I go use the restroom?"

ME "Class just began. Ask me again in thirty minutes."

HER (Quietly) "It's a girl thing."

ME "You just had your girl thing two weeks ago. Nice try."

HER "Wow. You have a good memory."

ME "I've got a girlfriend. I *have* to memorize these things."

THE DANCE

GRADE ELEVEN STUDENT "Sir, can you teach me how to dance?"
ME "Maybe. I can teach you how to move that."

I point to his feet.

ME "But you have to teach yourself how to move that."

I point to his heart.

HIM "Maybe I'll just take lessons at the community centre."

HITLER

GRADE ELEVEN STUDENT "Sir, what was Hitler's last name?"
ME "You serious?"
HIM "Oh. No, of course not. Just kidding."
ME "Tell me then."
HIM "Tell you what?"
ME "What was Hitler's last name?"

His friends start laughing.

HIM "Hey, he's so evil, he doesn't deserve to have his name
memorized."
ME "Nice."

CHOKED UP

I start choking on some water and coughing violently in the middle of a lesson. The students are just watching me, befuddled.

GRADE EIGHT STUDENT "Sir, are you all right?"

I continue coughing.

HER "Are you okay? Are you choking?"

I'm still coughing, moving to the sink to grab a glass of water.

HER "Do you need help? Do you want help? Sir?!"

I've finally stopped.

ME "Didn't you say you want to be a doctor one day?"
HER "Yeah. I asked good questions, right?"

ACCIDENTAL EDUCATION

GRADE NINE STUDENT "Sir, what do you think of my nails?"

She holds her newly painted nails towards me.

ME "You asking me because I'm Korean?"
HER "Huh?"
ME "Never mind."
HER "I don't get it."
ME "Forget it. I was kidding."
HER "Are Koreans good at nails? I thought Koreans did laundry stuff."
ME "Oh boy."

THANKSGIVING

GRADE TWELVE STUDENT "Sir, why do we celebrate Thanksgiving?"

ME "To remind ourselves to be thankful for everything we have."

HIM "You mean like crime, gang violence and war?"

ME "I'm guessing you never get to say grace at Thanksgiving dinner."

EMERGENCY

I've caught a grade ten student texting in class, so I've confiscated his cellphone.

HIM "That's so not fair, sir."

ME "How's it not fair? You knew the rules, and those rules apply to everyone equally."

HIM "How do you know it wasn't an emergency?"

ME "It's an emergency, so you decided to stay at school?"

HIM "I didn't say it was a big emergency."

ME "And you were laughing as you were texting."

HIM "It was a funny emergency."

OUTDOOR EDUCATION

Preparing grade eight students for our outdoor education program ...

STUDENT "Sir, what if a bear eats us?"

ME "I highly doubt it will eat all of us."

HIM "Maybe it will eat only you because you have the most meat on you."

ME "If you're lucky."

HIM "And you're probably too old to be fast anymore. Is your back still bad?"

ME "That's it. You're carrying all the beef jerky."

ME DAY

ME "Where were you last class?"

GRADE TWELVE STUDENT "I took a me day."

ME "Really? A *me day*?"

HIM "Yeah. It's a day where I celebrate me."

ME "How did you celebrate?"

HIM "Like any holiday."

ME "You slept in."

HIM "Yup."

PICTURE PERFECT

GRADE TWELVE STUDENT "Sir, can we see a photo of your girlfriend?"

ME "No."

HER "I'll show you a picture of my boyfriend."

ME "Why would I need to see that? I taught him last year."

HER "He looks different this year."

FRIENDS AGAIN

GRADE EIGHT STUDENT "Sir, just want to let you know that Sandra and I are best friends again."

ME "I didn't know you had stopped being friends."

HER "We had a big argument last week because Courtenay started saying some stuff about me, so we weren't friends, but then Sandra realized Courtenay's a big liar, so we made up and are friends again."

ME "Okay. But why are you telling me this?"

HER "Can I move my seat next to Sandra again?"

ME "Can you please just jump to your request next time?"

BFF

GRADE EIGHT STUDENT "Sir, who's your BFF?"

ME "My what?"

HER "Are you serious? *BFF*. Best friend forever."

ME "Really? That's a saying? Kids actually use that term?"

HER "What's wrong with it?"

ME "Let's just say that if I ever went up to another grown man and asked him to be my BFF, I wouldn't blame him if he punched me in the face."

HER "Well, then he's not your BFF."

TIME WASTED

GRADE ELEVEN STUDENT "Sir, how did you write essays if you didn't have computers in high school?"

ME "We used typewriters or wrote by hand."

HIM "How about research?"

ME "Books and libraries."

HIM "So you spent, like, hours at libraries?"

ME "As long as it took to do my research."

HIM "Man, your generation wasted so much time doing simple things."

ME "So what do you do with all your free time?"

HIM "I don't know. Hang out?"

WITH STYLE

GRADE EIGHT STUDENT "Sir, why don't you use your computer projector?"

ME "I like using the board. Nothing wrong with good old-fashioned writing."

HER "But it looks nicer on the computer."

ME "Oh. I never thought of that. Would you also like me to decorate the room so that it's a bit homier?"

HER "Now you're talking."

TOUGH TIMES

GRADE ELEVEN STUDENT "Sir, if you didn't have cellphones when you were our age, how did you talk to friends on the phone, especially girls?"

ME "We rarely talked too long on the phone back then because everyone's parents would answer the phone first. Plus, everyone had only one line to share with the whole family, so no one could hog the line."

HER "That sounds horrible."

ME "I just realized this is my generation's walked-barefoot-to-school-in-the-snow story."

HER "What?"

ME "Nothing."

TOUGH TIMES, PART 2

GRADE ELEVEN STUDENT "Sir, what did you do when you went out with friends back in the eighties? How did other friends reach you?"

ME "They didn't. You were committed to the friends who agreed to meet you that night. Those who were noncommittal—well, too bad."

HER "But what if your night started to suck? Or you were bored?"

ME "Kids didn't get bored as easily back then."

HER "No way. That can't be true."

ME "Have you ever heard of *Pong*?"

1492

GRADE TEN STUDENT "Sir, when did Columbus get here?"

ME "Remember: 'In fourteen hundred and ninety-two, Columbus sailed the ocean blue.'"

HIM "Fifteen hundred and ninety-two. Sixteen hundred and ninety-two. It all fits!"

ME "Just ... remember the date."

SITCOM

GRADE ELEVEN STUDENT "Sir, you should write a sitcom about us."

ME *"Welcome Back, Kotter. Head of the Class. Hangin' with Mr. Cooper.* It's been done."

HIM "What were those about?"

ME "A loving teaching who does everything to help his students succeed."

HIM "How about a high school teacher who tries to act young for his cool students, but he's not? That's funny, right?"

ME "How about a student who thinks he's going to pass English, but he doesn't. That's funnier, right?"

CANADIAN THANKSGIVING

GRADE ELEVEN STUDENT "Sir, why do Canadians have Thanksgiving on a different day than the United States?"

ME "I don't really know. I think it has something to do with how ours is mainly to celebrate the harvest, but the American holiday is tied to Puritan traditions brought over from England."

HER "Are you guessing?"

ME "Just relaying what I've heard. Why don't you ask your history teacher?"

HER "She's not here right now. You are."

ME "I suppose I should be thankful for that?"

HER "Yes. Count your blessings, sir."

GRANDE BRANDING

One of my grade ten students walks into class holding a large green drink.

ME "Wow. What is that?"

HER "Seriously, sir? You've never seen this?"

ME "No."

HER "It's a green tea Frappuccino. Don't you ever go to Starbucks?"

ME "Sometimes."

HER "And what do you order?"

ME "A coffee."

HER "But what kind?"

ME "Usually medium roast."

HER "That's so boring. You should try ordering something different. Something unique."

ME "Unique? At *Starbucks*?"

Her friends start giggling.

HER "I don't get it."

DON'T MAKE A SISYFUSS

GRADE NINE STUDENT "Sir, do we have to do work today?"

ME "What do you think?"

HIM "Yeah?"

ME "Yes."

HIM "Sorry. *Yes*."

INSTRUCTIONS

GRADE ELEVEN STUDENT "Sir, may I use the restroom?"

ME "Class just started. Why didn't you use it during the break?"

HIM "I didn't have to go then. I have to now."

ME "Well, let me finish giving the instructions so I don't have to repeat myself."

HIM "Sir, when have you ever had to not repeat yourself to me?"

ME "Go ahead."

HIM "Thanks!"

THE KING AND I

HER "You told us at the beginning of the year that we're allowed to challenge you on ideas."

ME "Elvis is not an idea. He's a fact."

TOTALLY YOU

One of my grade nine students approaches my desk and shows me a drawing.

HER "Sir, that's you."

ME "Really?"

I mock appraise it like an art dealer.

ME "That is excellent!"

HER "You think so? You're not just saying that?"

ME "No. It looks just like me."

HER "Thanks. I made sure to make the eyes Asian like yours."

ME "Thanks."

SHE'S NUMBER ONE

I catch one of my grade nine students giving another student the middle finger. I quietly summon her to my desk.

ME "What was that?"

HER "What?"

ME "Why did you give her the finger?"

HER "It's nothing."

ME "Seems like something. She didn't look like she appreciated it."

HER "Trust me, she had it coming."

ME "I can't imagine any context where flashing her your middle finger will resolve the situation."

HER "You ever been a teenage girl?"

ME "No."

HER "That's why you can't imagine it."

EDM

GRADE TEN STUDENT "Sir, do you like EDM?"

ME "What's EDM?"

She turns to her friends and rolls her eyes. They giggle at me.

HER "It's electronic dance music."

ME "We used to just call it music. Let me show you something."

I start walking towards my computer.

HER "Are you going to make us listen to dance music from your time to show us how much better your music was compared to ours?"

ME "What makes you think that?"

She sighs.

HER "You were about to load up some YouTube video of some eighties synth band."

ME "How'd you know?"

HER "Sir, you do the same thing every time the topic of music comes up. It's so predictable."

ME "Like electronic dance music?"

Some boys start laughing.

HER "Like your jokes."

The class erupts with laughter.

ME "You win."

WHITE LIE

GRADE ELEVEN STUDENT "Sir, are you Facebook friends with your parents?"

ME "No."

HER "How did you swing that?"

ME "My mother asked me how to get on 'the Facebook' and I told her there's a monthly fee. So she didn't join."

HER "That's awful!"

ME "Or I could have told her the truth and have her all over my wall."

HER "So it was a white lie."

THE WAVE

I started a breakdance club after school. It became the most popular extracurricular activity in our school and was packed with students from every grade. This day, I was teaching the basics to a new group.

STUDENT "Sir, I'm not getting this."

He's referring to the wave. I take his arm to demonstrate how to move it.

ME "You have to imagine a current passing through your body. Start at the fingers, and then the wrist. Then the elbow, shoulders. See? Like that. Here."

I wrap his fingers in mine and pass a wave into his arm. It works.

ME "It's like I'm passing energy from me to you."
HIM "I bet this worked on all the ladies."
ME "You trying to make this awkward?"
HIM "Sorry, sir. I really don't know anything about ladies."

HALLOWEEN COSTUME

GRADE ELEVEN STUDENT "Great costume, sir."
ME "I'm not wearing a costume."
HIM "Oh. I thought you were a waiter."

GARDYLOO!

The subject in class today is the sudden growth of European towns before the Industrial Revolution.

ME "In Old Edinburgh, residents of tenements used to shout 'Gardyloo!' to warn passersby of feces and urine about to be emptied out windows."

STUDENT "Gross. So they'd hang their butts out the windows?"

ME "They used chamber pots."

HIM "Oh. That's not as nasty."

HAIRCUT

I walk into my English 9 class.

STUDENT "Hey, sir, you got a haircut."

ME "Yeah, thanks."

HER "Why are you thanking me?"

ME "Oh, sorry. I assumed it was a compliment."

HER "Nope."

ME "So you were just voicing your observation."

HER "Yup."

I let the awkwardness linger. Students start giggling. She doesn't break.

ME "That's it?"

HER "Yeah."

ME "Okay, then. Nice chatting with you."

BREATHLESS

I lean forward to help one of my English 10 students with her assignment. I begin explaining when she interrupts by leaning away and making a sour face.

HER "Sir, you need some gum."
ME "My breath that bad?"
HER "It's the coffee. I hate coffee breath."
ME "I don't have gum. Sorry."
HER "Then can you stand farther away?"

She waves a hand to shoo me away. Some of the kids around us have started giggling. I walk all the way to the back of the room, and then turn and continue explaining the assignment very loudly. She is laughing along with everyone. I keep at it for a good minute.

HER "You don't have to stand that far away, sir!"
ME "No, no, my breath is awful. I'm hideous! How did my mother love me?"
HER "Okay, you can come back. It's not that bad."

I jog back to my initial spot but keep my head far enough away.

ME "How's this?"

She sniffs the air.

HER "That will do."

HALLOWEEN

GRADE TEN STUDENT "Sir, what are you dressing as for
Halloween?"

ME "I'm thinking Bruce Lee."

HIM "So you're not dressing up?"

He starts laughing. I whip my head around and stare at him. My
jaws tighten and I look at him intently, with my head slightly tilted
downward, never breaking eye contact.

He has stopped laughing.

HIM "I ... I'm sorry, sir. I was only joking."

I break into a smile.

ME "That was my Bruce Lee. Pretty good, eh?"

HIM "Please don't ever do that again, sir."

TOO MATURE

One of my grade eight students looks like he's having a bad morning.

ME   "What's going on, mister?"

HIM   "I missed trick-or-treating yesterday."

ME   "Why's that?"

HIM   "My dad says I'm too old now."

ME   "Yeah, to be honest, you do seem a bit too mature for that. You're not really a kid anymore."

HIM   "But my costume still fits."

ME   "You know what? You're going to start finding that you're too old for a lot of things, but in exchange for that, you'll get to start doing a bunch of stuff only teenagers get to do."

HIM   "That sounds awful."

WHOSE HAPPINESS?

GRADE ELEVEN STUDENT   "Sir, don't your parents want you to get married one day?"

ME   "Of course."

HER   "So, why don't you?"

ME   "My partner and I are very happy the way things are, thank you."

HER   "But don't you ever think about your parents' happiness, or is it always about your own?"

ME   "Did my mother send you?"

WHAT DID THAT WHIPPERSNAPPER SAY?

In English 9, on the topic of 9/11 ...

STUDENT 1 "They're going to rebuild the Twin Towers."
STUDENT 2 "They're rebuilding the what?"
STUDENT 3 "The *Titanic*."
STUDENT 2 "Why the hell would they rebuild the *Titanic*?"
ME "It's like an old folks' home in here."

MISREAD

GRADE TEN STUDENT "Sometimes, sir, you're so hard to read."
ME "You don't enjoy the classics?"

Blank stare from her.

ME "Got it."

IT'S WASTED ON THE YOUNG

GRADE NINE STUDENT "Sir, what do you use in your hair? Gel?"
ME "No, I use a pomade. Why?"
HIM "I like the way it sticks up."
ME "Thank you."
HIM "I like it. It's like, you're old, but you still try hard to stay young."
ME "Kind of like how you're trying to pass my course?"

WEEKEND PLANS

GRADE TWELVE STUDENT "Sir, what are you doing this weekend?"
ME "Nothing much. Relaxing."

HIM "So ... you're drinking with friends."

ME "Mind your own business."

HIM (To his buddy) "I told you."

FAVOURITE PART

After reading a short story together in English 10 class ...

ME "What part of the story did you like?"

A student raises his hand.

ME "Yes?"

HIM "The end."

ME "Why?"

HIM "It ended."

BIEBER FEVER

A grade nine student is telling me about her experience at the Justin Bieber concert.

HER "It was amazing. And you could tell he was loving it. All the screaming girls."

ME "Who were they screaming at?"

HER "Who do you think? Justin."

ME "Oh, sorry. I got mixed up cuz you know what I call that?"

HER "What?"

ME "A typical Friday night."

I raise my hand for a high-five. Nothing. Just an angry girl's stare.

SMELL IT UP

There's a commotion in English 10 class. One of the guys is waving his hand furiously in front of his face.

STUDENT 1 "Sir, he farted!"

STUDENT 2 "Relax."

ME (To Student 2) "You know you can smell up your own gas particles so that no one else smells them?"

STUDENT 2 "Really?"

He now starts inhaling deeply through his nose.

ME "Okay, I have to stop you."

STUDENT 2 "Why?"

ME "You're making me question why I'm here."

MR MISOGYNY

GRADE ELEVEN STUDENT "Sir, what's a misogynist?"

ME "Someone who hates women."

HIM "That's stupid. I don't hate women."

ME "Who called you a misogynist?"

HIM "Some chick my sister knows. She's the misogynist. A man misogynist."

I pull up a chair.

ME "Have a seat."

HOLY, HOLY, HOLY

ME "The prose came from an old English hymn."

STUDENT "A man?"

ME "Yes."

HIM "So ... an English *man*."

ME "Yes."

HIM "You could just say Englishman."

ME "What are you talking about?"

STUDENT 2 "Sir, I think he's confusing English *hymn* with H-I-M."

ME "Really? No ... right?"

STUDENT 1 "Um ... yeah. Sorry."

GAY MARRIAGE

GRADE EIGHT STUDENT "Sir, why is gay marriage bad?"

ME "It's not."

HIM "Then why does my dad say it is?"

ME "Oh boy."

GODWIN'S LAW

GRADE TWELVE STUDENT "Well, yeah, Hitler was wrong, but ..."

ME "I'm going to stop you right there."

HIM "Why?"

ME "It's my experience that that sentence never ends well."

HIM "I don't get it."

ME "Without saying it, think about what you were about to say."

HIM "Yeah."

ME "Now, look around the room at everyone's faces. How do you think everyone's going to take whatever you were about to say?"

He thinks for a few seconds.

HIM "Good call, sir."

IT'S IN THE GENES

GRADE TEN STUDENT "Sir, if you ever had a son, would you want him to be like me?"

ME "No."

HIM "What?? Why?"

ME "Because you never listen to me."

HIM "I'll listen to you! I swear!"

ME "Okay. Let's see how you do this week, and if you're better at listening, then I'll set up an alternate reality and adopt you."

HIM "Cool."

HIS BUDDY (To him) "I wouldn't adopt you."

THERE IS A LIGHT THAT SOMETIMES WENT OUT

GRADE TWELVE STUDENT "Sir, did you have a girlfriend in high school?"

ME "No."

HIM "Did you date?"

ME "Yes."

HIM "Why didn't you keep dating them?"

ME "Because I ran out of money after the first dates."

STUDENT 2 "Man, you weren't too bright at our age, were you, sir?"

JUST CALL ME BRUCE

GRADE TEN STUDENT "Sir, do you like Bruce Lee?"

ME "Are you asking because I'm Asian?"

HIM "Um ... maybe. Why? Is that bad?"

ME "Isn't that a stereotype that all Asian men like Bruce Lee?"

HIM "I guess so. Sorry, sir."

ME "Oh, don't apologize. I love him!"

FACEBOOK FRIENDS

GRADE TWELVE STUDENT "Sir, I invited you to be my Facebook friend last week. Why won't you add me?"

ME "I told you: I don't add students until they've graduated."

HIM "Why not?"

ME "It's just my policy. I would find it awkward."

HIM "Cuz of all the sexy stuff?"

ME "Never mind. New policy: I'm never adding you."

THE SECRET TO HAPPINESS

GRADE TEN STUDENT "Sir, do you know the secret to happiness?"

ME "No."

HIM "A happy penis! Get it? Happiness? Happy penis?"

ME "Yeah, yeah, I got it."

HIM "You did? Why aren't you laughing?"

ME "Because I don't get it anymore."

HIM "What?"

ME "Never mind."

NOT QUITE

ME "All right, people, please put away your books. We have a guest speaker."

GIRL "What's he talking about?"

ME "You'll see."

HER "Is he going to talk about cheese?"

ME "Why? Why would he talk about cheese?"

HER "I don't know. Just had a feeling."

ME "Today, your feelings are way off."

MIDDLE NAME

GRADE NINE STUDENT "Sir, what's your first name?"

ME "Paul."

HIM "Hey, that's my uncle's name."

ME "Cool."

HIM "What's your middle name?"

ME "It's in Korean."

HIM "Oh. That's probably not my uncle's middle name."

HE'LL BE BACK

GRADE NINE STUDENT "Sir, do you ever worry about losing your job? Like, when computers and robots take over?"

ME "I doubt you'd want a robot teaching you."

HER "Why not?"

ME "Because something will eventually go wrong and someone from the future will have to come back to fix it all and you'll be caught in the middle of it."

HER "What?"

ME "See? You're not ready."

RACISM

One of my Chinese grade ten students approaches me after school.

HIM "Sir, have you ever experienced racism?"

ME "Sadly, yes."

HIM "What did you do?"

ME "It's always different. I used to let it slide, but when I was old enough to find my voice, I stood up for myself. Did something happen to you today?"

HIM "Someone called me a Chinaman."

ME "That must have hurt."

HIM "Has anyone ever called you a Chinaman?"

ME "Yes."

HIM "Did you get mad?"

ME "Of course. But mainly because I'm Korean."

TRUST

GRADE TWELVE STUDENT "Sir, can I get an extension on my essay?"

ME "Sure."

HIM "Don't you want to know why?"

ME "Well, there's no reason not to trust you, so no."

HIM "Wow. Thanks!"

He's about to walk away but then returns.

HIM "Um, I didn't really have a reason, though. I just procrastinated."

ME "And *that's* why I trust you."

HIM "Cool!"

PENMANSHIP

GRADE TEN STUDENT "Sir, may I borrow a pen?"

ME "Where's the pen I gave you last time?"

HIM "I don't know."

ME "Well, I'm going to need collateral this time. Give me your cellphone."

HIM "No way! My cellphone's worth way more than your pen."

ME "Right now it isn't."

He mulls it over for a few seconds before reluctantly exchanging his phone for a pen.

ME "You are the worst haggler. Why didn't you just ask one of your friends here for a pen?"

HIM "I don't trust them with my phone."

PICKY

I overhear the middle of a conversation between two boys in English 10 ...

STUDENT "Your dad is so closed-minded, man. So what if she's Chinese? What if she was Japanese? Or Korean? Or—"

ME "Or German?"

HIM "Oh, he's only into Asian girls, sir."

1984

The grade twelve English class has just started reading George Orwell's *1984*.

STUDENT "Sir, have you seen the movie version of this?"

ME "Yeah. It's not bad."

HIM   "Yeah, that actor is a pretty good Winston. It's like how I imagined Winston to be."

ME   "Yeah, he's a fine actor."

HIM   "And I like how the director kept all the main points of the book."

ME   "How do you know? We just started reading the book."

HIM   "Oh, I just assumed, you know, that, like ..."

ME   "Are you trying to find out if the movie wholly captures the novel so that you don't have to read it?"

HIM   "No way, man! That's so ... *1984*."

ME   "What does that even mean?"

HIM   "Okay. I'll read it."

NOT EVEN CLOSE

I'm breaking up an argument in English 8.

ME   "What's going on here?"

PATRICK   "They're calling me Patricia!"

MARTIN   "That's cuz you were calling me Martina! And you called Warren Wendy!"

ME   "Wendy?"

PATRICK   "I couldn't think of anything closer."

DOGS

GRADE NINE STUDENT   "Sir, did you know pigs are as smart as dogs?"

ME   "I have heard that."

HIM   "That's crazy! I have a dog. I could never imagine eating him."

ME   "You thinking about quitting pork?"

HIM "Maybe. But I love bacon. And ribs. And hot dogs."

ME "You've got yourself quite the quandary there."

HIM "Sir, you're Korean, right?"

ME "Yes."

HIM "Have you ever—"

ME "No."

HIM "Oh, okay."

FAVOURITE SONG

My English 9 students have to write about their favourite song.

STUDENT "Sir, I can't remember the title of that Michael Jackson song I like."

ME "He's got a lot of songs. Pick another one."

HER "But I love this one."

ME "Can you hum it or something? How does it go?"

HER (Singing) "You are not alone—"

I wait for it to kick in. Nothing.

ME "It's 'You Are Not Alone.'"

HER "Oh yeah!"

OHIO

STUDENT 1 "What does Ohio mean?"

STUDENT 2 "I think it's a place in Hawaii."

STUDENT 1 "Why would Ohio be named after another place?"

STUDENT 2 "I think it's like a New England thing. It's like England, but different."

STUDENT 1 "But then shouldn't it be New Ohio?"

STUDENT 2 "Sir, what does—"

ME "Don't ask me. You two have it covered."

PASSWORD

GRADE TEN STUDENT "Sir, I don't remember my password to log on to the computer."

ME "Have you tried your name and birthdate?"

HIM "No."

ME "Why not?"

HIM "I know it wasn't my name."

ME "How are you so sure of that?"

HIM "It was something dirty. I just don't know what."

ME "I can't help you anymore."

COOL

GRADE TWELVE STUDENT "Sir, it's too hot in here to study."

ME "Why don't you take off your jacket, then? Or your hat?"

HIM "Nah. This is all a package. It's a look."

ME "In my day, guys wanted to look cool, not warm."

HIM "Warm is cool now."

ME "Really?"

HIM "I don't know. I just came up with that."

ME "That's cool."

HIM "Thanks!"

WANTON!

In English 11 …

ME "This character shows a wanton disregard for his co-workers. Why does he behave like this?"

STUDENT "He's eating soup?"

ME "What?"

HIM "Chinese soup."

ME "Not *wonton*. Wanton."

HIM "Oh. Then I don't know."

WORLD'S OLDEST DIS

STUDENT "Sir, were there prostitutes in Shakespeare's time?"

ME "Yes. Why?"

HIM (Pointing to a line in his book) "He's looking for one or something."

ME "'What ho,'" means 'You there.'"

HIM "Oh. Okay, that makes more sense."

FOUL BALL

We have just begun *Macbeth* in English 11 …

ME "So, what does the phrase 'Fair is foul and foul is fair' mean?"

STUDENT "It's like when you hit a foul ball but the umpire calls it fair, but you know it crossed the foul line."

ME "Did you read the first act for homework?"

HIM "Yeah."

ME "Then what are the witches trying to say?"

HIM "The witches ... are saying ... that you can't tell right
from wrong sometimes."

ME "You are a great guesser."

HIM "Thanks."

SPACE AND PACE

One of my grade ten students is having problems with her boyfriend
and we're in the middle of hashing it out.

GRADE TEN STUDENT "It's like he gets so mad if I don't answer his
texts right away."

ME "You don't have to do what he says. Why not let him stew in it?
Make him wait. Let him know you're worth waiting for."

HER "But what if he breaks up with me?"

ME "Two words: 'space' and 'pace.' If he won't respect *your* space
and *your* pace, you need to let him know *his* place."

I snap my fingers over my head with authority.

HER "Whoa. That's good!"

ME "In the eighties, we needed everything to rhyme or it wasn't cool."

SMART PLANNER

GRADE TEN STUDENT "Sir, do we have to use our school day
planners?"

ME "No. You can use your smartphone to organize your studies."

HIM "Cool."

ME "Mind showing me your calendar app so I can see how you
organize your projects?"

HIM "I haven't got to that stage yet."

ME "It's already November. Where have you been keeping track of your projects?"

He smiles and points at his head.

ME "How much memory does that take up?"

HIM "None."

GROWING FRUIT

GRADE EIGHT STUDENT "Sir, how do you grow a pair?"

ME "What's that?"

He's confused that I'm confused. He points to a pear sitting on my desk.

ME "Oh, a *pear*."

HIM "What do you think I said?"

ME "Nothing."

THEY'RE NUTS

I see two of my grade eight students in the hallway during lunch sitting wide-legged about five metres from each other. They are quickly rolling a volleyball at each other, aiming between each other's legs.

ME "Gentlemen, mind if I ask what's going on?"

STUDENT 1 "We're playing nut ball, sir."

ME "Ah, I see."

STUDENT 2 "We're trying to hit each other in the n—"

ME "I can see what you're trying to do. My question was actually: *Why?*"

They exchange glances with each other. They shrug.

STUDENT 1 "Because we can."

ME "Okay, then. Carry on."

Some things you just walk away from.

WRONG NUMBER

A grade nine student is waiting for the class to leave so that he can talk to me in private.

ME "What's up?"

HIM "Sir, can you call my mother and ask her to give me back my phone?"

ME "Why do you want *me* to call?"

HIM "Because my parents like you. If you ask them, they'll listen to you. Tell them how I need it for work and stuff."

ME "Why was your phone taken away?"

HIM "They said I was texting too much."

ME "Sorry, but I don't think it's my place to tell your parents how to raise you."

HIM "You're not doing that. You're only telling them I need my phone."

ME "But you don't."

HIM "I do!"

ME "I got through school without a cellphone and look how I
turned out."

HIM "But that was like fifty years ago, so none of your friends had
cellphones either."

ME "Fifty years? Really?"

HIM "Sorry. Forty?"

IN THE MEMBRANE

It's after school and I'm driving three of my junior rugby players to
a game across town. I have Echo and the Bunnymen playing on my
car stereo. The boys are all oddly quiet.

ME "So, how was school today?"

A round of mumbles and shrugs.

ME "You guys ready to kick some butt?"

STUDENT 1 "Sir, what is this?"

ME "Sorry?"

HIM "This."

ME "Oh, my music? This is one of the greatest bands to ever come
out of the eighties: Echo and the Bunnymen. This is called
'Bring on the Dancing Horses.' When I was your age, we used
to—"

STUDENT 2 "Do you have anything else? Like hip hop?"

ME (Incredulous) "Do I have hip hop?"

I change up the CD. It's taking a while for me to cue my song.
The boys are unimpressed.

The song's finally ready.

ME "Hip hop, you say? Well, an insane question deserves …"

I hit play.

ME (High-pitched nasal voice) "An insane answer."

The Beastie Boys comes on. The students look confused.

ME "Sorry. I thought I had Cypress Hill coming on. It would have made more sense."

ALL THEM

In the middle of a lesson with my English 11 class.

ME "Why do we use the term 'heartbreak'? Why 'break'? Why not 'pain' or 'sting'?"

STUDENT "Because it leaves you feeling shattered."

Everyone's heads turn towards him. They obviously like his answer. And he doesn't usually give profound answers.

ME "That's a good word for that. 'Shattered.' What made you use that word?"

HIM "That's what the ladies tell me it feels like when I leave them in the morning."

The boys in the class explode with laughter. He's getting high-fives. The girls are rolling their eyes and laughing *at* him.

ME "Do any of the *ladies* here have something to say to that?"

A bunch of hands shoot into the air.
The student who answered is shrinking in his seat.

HIM "I take it back! I take it back! Mercy!"

Everyone's laughing now. Some girls are muttering something to him, quietly laying down some smack talk, and it's making him turn red with embarrassment.

ME "How does your ego feel?"
HIM "Shattered, sir!"

ZOMBIES AND MARRIAGE

Near the end of my English 10 class, two students are hanging out by my desk.

STUDENT 1 "Sir, would you marry a zombie if you loved her and she had total self-awareness?"
STUDENT 2 "Dude, he already told us he's divorced and doesn't feel the need to remarry."
STUDENT 1 "So? What does that have to do with this?"
STUDENT 2 "Because why would he marry a zombie if he won't even marry a human?"
STUDENT 1 "That's like apples and oranges, man."
STUDENT 2 "But the institution's the same."
STUDENT 1 "Sir? What do you think?"
ME "I think you guys have this covered. Don't let me stop you."

YOUTUBER

After school one of my grade nine students is at one of the classroom computers. She looks deflated.

ME "What's going on?"

HER "Someone wrote something mean on my YouTube video."

ME "May I see?"

She turns the screen towards me. I read.

ME "I'd say it's more stupid than mean."

HER "What if he's right?"

ME "Have you ever commented on a stranger's YouTube video?"

HER "Yes."

ME "What did you write?"

HER "I just wanted to let the person know how good the video was."

ME "Would you ever leave a nasty comment?"

HER "No."

ME "Why not?"

HER "I don't know. It just feels mean."

ME "But this guy took the time out of his day to write this nasty stuff. Can you picture the kind of person this is?"

HER "Not really."

ME "Well, do you think I would ever write something like that?"

HER "No."

ME "Do you think any of your best friends would write something like that?"

HER "No."

ME "So, none of your favourite people would write like that. So, if you met this person in real life, do you think you'd like him? Do you think he'd be a cool person?"

HER "No way."
ME "Then?"

She thinks about it.

HER "Sir, may I swear for a second?"

I look around. No one is within earshot. I nod.
She looks at the screen.

HER "F*ck you, Screendevil666!"

I quietly, happily watch as she breathes a sigh of relief.

ME "Better?"
HER "Way better."
ME "Good. Don't ever swear again in here."
HER (Beaming) "You got it, sir."

CO-OPERATIVE LEARNING

My grade eight students are in groups of four discussing an assignment. A debate in one of the groups starts to get heated and voices are raised.

ME "Hey, guys. What's going on here?"
STUDENT 1 "We're fighting."
ME "I can hear that. Who's the designated referee today?"

They all point at another student.

ME "Why aren't you refereeing?"
STUDENT 2 "I'm not sure when to step in."

ME "Okay. How about when your group members start yelling at each other, you raise your yellow card?"

STUDENT 2 "Okay."

ME "All right. Let's do a little replay of the foul, okay? So, who started the argument?"

They all point at him.

STUDENT 2 "I'm not the best referee."

DECEMBER

SEMIOTICS ... KIND OF

ME "What do you like about the story?"

GRADE NINE STUDENT "I like how the words help you picture what's going on."

ME "Yes, that's how writing works."

STRESSFUL SITUATION

GRADE EIGHT STUDENT "Sir, may I play with your balls?"

ME "What?"

HIM "You know, your balls."

He cups his hands upwards and makes squeezing motions with his fingers.

ME "Oh, the stress balls."

HIM "Yeah."

ME "Next time, just ask for the *stress balls*, and don't make that motion with your hands."

(PARA)NORMAL

GRADE EIGHT STUDENT "Sir, I'm not going to be here Thursday."

ME "Why?"

HIM "I'm going to be sick."

ME "What are you, psychic?"

HIM (Yelling) "No, I said *SICK*!"

IT'S BEEN A DECADE

During English 10 ...

ME "What are some of your favourite drinks?"

STUDENT "Milkshakes. My mom makes the best ones."

ME "Oh yeah? I make a pretty mean one. In fact, mine brings all the boys to the yard."

Blank stares from everyone.

ME "Milkshakes. My milkshake brings all the boys to the yard."

Nothing.

ME "Are you serious? *Already*?"

RICHES

GRADE ELEVEN STUDENT "Sir, are you rich?"

ME "I'm a public school teacher. What do you think?"

HIM "But you said you have another job, too."

ME "And do rich people work two jobs?"

HIM "Ah, right."

COHABITATION

GRADE TWELVE STUDENT "Sir, how did you end up living with your girlfriend? Like, how did you know it was time to live together?"

ME "I'm not sure. It was like a slumber party that kept on going."

STUDENT 2 "Yeah, my mom's boyfriend is sleeping over a lot. I can hear them from my room and—"

ME "Moving on!"

NOT A BEAUTIFUL MIND

GRADE TEN STUDENT "Sir, when did you lose your virginity?"

ME "That's none of your business."

HIM "Okay. Then when was your first kiss?"

ME "Ah, that I can share. It was in fifth grade."

HIM "Okay, so mathematically, you probably went all the way by grade seven."

ME "What are you getting in math?"

HIM "A C-minus."

ME "Figures."

TOO MUCH INFORMATION

GRADE EIGHT STUDENT "Sir, may I drink my juice during class?"

ME "Yes."

HER "Thanks, cuz I need the sugars cuz I'm menstruating right now and ..."

ME "What part of *YES* do you not understand?"

NORTH AND SOUTH

GRADE ELEVEN STUDENT "Sir, are you Chinese?"

ME "I'm Korean."

HIM "North or South Korean?"

ME "Yes, I'm North Korean. I escaped from a prison camp in my teens, made my way over to Seoul, where I worked on losing my accent before moving to North America."

HIM "Wow. You should write a book about that."

APP—TITUDE

GRADE TEN STUDENT "Sir, do you have any games on your
smartphone?"

ME "Just a few."

I hand him my phone. He looks through my apps.

HIM "Wow. These suck. You don't play a lot of games, do you?"

ME "No. I spend most of my time trying to decipher what you're
trying to say in your essays."

A CHRISTMAS MIRACLE

Grade eights walk into my classroom during my lesson prep time.

STUDENT "Sir, may we sing you a Christmas carol?"

ME "Sorry, gentlemen. I've got sensitive ears."

HIM "Hey, that's not nice."

ME "I mean, they're *sensitive*. If you sing too beautifully, I'll cry."

HIM "Oh, okay. Next room, guys."

FACEBOOK SECURITY

During a lesson on social media security and privacy for teens, I use
my Facebook account to access one of my student's profiles in front
of her.

ME "Look, Jennifer. Your profile is totally open. You've got no
privacy settings."

HER FRIEND (Motioning to me) "Yeah, Jen, you don't want any
old perv creeping on you."

ME "Yeah. Hey!"

SEXTUAL ANALYSIS

During a presentation on social media safety and privacy to a grade nine class, the police officer guest speaker moves on to sexting.

OFFICER "You don't want to take a picture of your junk and send it out there, cuz it's out there forever."

STUDENT "Can you advertise it on Craigslist?"

OFFICER (After a confused silence) "Why ... what?"

ME "Junk. He's literally talking about junk."

The officer looks over the student who is patiently waiting for an answer.

OFFICER "Let me start that that one over."

CHRISTMAS CONFUSION

GRADE EIGHT STUDENT "Sir, when did you stop believing in Santa Claus?"

ME "I can't recall. I don't remember ever believing in Santa Claus."

HER "So weren't you afraid of going to hell?"

ME "You're thinking of the other Christmas guy."

ETIQUETTE

GRADE TWELVE STUDENT "Sir, my girlfriend says that when we're on a sidewalk, I'm supposed to walk on the curbside. Is that true?"

ME "Yup."

HIM "Why's that?"

ME "Because she says so."

HIM "I hear that."

TWITTER PARTY

GRADE TWELVE STUDENT "Sir, follow me on Twitter."

ME "Why in the world do you want a teacher following you?"

HIM "I need more followers."

ME "How many do you have?"

HIM "About nine."

ME "Isn't that like throwing a small party of your friends and then inviting me along? Wouldn't that be weird?"

HIM "Not if you bring booze."

ME "You're losing the metaphor."

TWITTER AFTER-PARTY

THE SAME GRADE TWELVE STUDENT FROM YESTERDAY "Sir, you didn't follow me on Twitter."

ME "All your tweets are just your horoscopes. That's it. You've got to give people a reason to follow you."

HIM "What's better than horoscopes?"

ME "Have you tried Myspace?"

NICE GIFT

STUDENT "Sir, what are you getting your girlfriend for Christmas?"

ME "Something nice."

HER "Diamonds?"

ME "I think we have different definitions of 'nice.'"

SERIOUS PLANS

I catch two grade nine girls writing a list.

ME "What are you doing?"

GIRL 1 "We're making a list of baby names."

ME "Either one of you expecting?"

GIRL 1 "Yeah, right! We're just thinking ahead."

ME "How about thinking ahead to college or something? I have pamphlets for most of them here."

GIRL 2 "Why do you have to turn this serious?"

ME "Sorry. I'll let you get back to planning babies instead."

GIRL 2 "Thanks."

DOLLA BILLZ

During English 11 ...

ME "A lot of you are probably feeling the pressure already of deciding what to do after graduation next year."

STUDENT "I'm gonna be a lifeguard."

ME "Yeah?"

HIM "Yeah, cuz I'll be drowning in dolla, dolla billz, y'all."

ME "Do lifeguards make that much money?"

HIM "No, I'm saying I'll be making so much money, it'll be like I'm drowning in the sea."

ME "But if *you're* the one drowning, shouldn't you make sure someone else is a licensed lifeguard? Your occupation becomes irrelevant, doesn't it?"

HIM "Man, you don't get it."

ME "Someone, help! This metaphor is drowning!"

THE CURE

During English 11 ...

STUDENT 1 "Sir, who were your favourite bands when you were in our grade?"

ME "At that time? Maybe U2, the Smiths, the Cure."

STUDENT 2 "What were they the cure for? Lame music?"

He gets a high-five from Student 1.

ME "If they were a cure for lame music, wouldn't that mean they make good music?"

STUDENT 2 "Um ..."

ME (To Student 1) "And you high-fived him."

STUDENT 1 "It was forced. I couldn't leave him hanging."

CHAIRS

GRADE TWELVE STUDENT "Sir, why do you get that sweet office chair and we have to sit in these crappy ones?"

ME "Yeah, it's pretty unfair."

HIM "Why don't we all get office chairs?"

ME "Who's going to pay for it?"

HIM "Taxpayers?"

ME "I doubt that would go over well with taxpayers."

HIM "We just have to be smart about it. Tell them the money's for books. They don't need to know the real reason."

ME "You're too young to be this corrupt."

HIM "I'm a product of our system."

INCONTINENCE

GRADE TEN STUDENT "Sir, Ryan says they sell diapers for adults."

ME "It's true. But don't call them diapers."

HIM "But why do adults need them?"

ME "It's for adult incontinence. It happens."

HIM "On land?"

ME "What?"

HIM "Only on land?"

ME "Incontinence. Not *in continents*."

HIM "I don't get it."

ME "Sometimes I feel like I'm the victim of a prank show."

CHRISTMAS CONFUSION

GRADE EIGHT STUDENT "Sir, were Jesus and Santa Claus friends?"

ME "Very funny."

HIM "So ... no?"

ME "Oh. You're serious."

YOUNG LOVE

One of my grade eight students has a crush on a girl.

HIM "I really like her, sir."

ME "That's great."

HIM "I think I'm going to stick this one out."

ME "How long you thinking?"

HIM "I don't know. At least three weeks."

YOUNG LOVE, PART 2

One of my grade eight students is filling me in on a girl he's been seeing.

HIM "I really like her, sir. Whenever we're together, we're like monkeys."

ME "I don't think I want to hear this."

HIM "Like, if I climb the monkey bars, she climbs them even higher."

ME "Oh."

PARENT—TEACHER INTERVIEWS

GRADE TEN STUDENT "Sir, my parents are coming in tonight to meet you."

ME "Yup. I can't wait."

HER "What are you going to say to them?"

ME "We're going to go over your marks, your behaviour, any concerns that we have. The usual."

HER "Is it good or bad?"

ME "I'm just going to be honest."

HER "I'm dead."

OH LORD ...

A new Chinese student has transferred into my English 9 class. He has only been in Canada for a few years.

HIM "Sir, what does gay lord mean?"

ME "Did someone call you that?"

HIM "Yes."

He tells me who it was.

ME   "He can be a bit of a bully. I'll talk to him."

HIM   "But what does it mean?"

ME   "Do you know what gay means?"

HIM   "Yes. I'm not gay."

ME   "Okay. Do you know what lord means?"

HIM   "No."

ME   "It's like a master. A king."

HIM   "Oh. So I am a gay king?"

ME   "Something like that."

HIM   "That is not so bad then."

DODGE

A small grade eight student is at my door during the break.

ME   "Hey, what's up?"

HIM   "Can I hang out here?"

ME   "Where are you supposed to be?"

HIM   "Gym."

ME   "I don't think your teacher will appreciate you skipping class."

He looks troubled.

ME   "What are you supposed to do today in gym?"

HIM   "Dodgeball."

ME   "Yeah, you can stay here."

REDO

GRADE ELEVEN STUDENT "Sir, I don't like my mark."

ME "Neither do I. You probably shouldn't have skipped out so often."

HIM "What can I do to change it?"

ME "You can't."

HIM "There must be some way."

ME "Well, there might be one way, but I don't know."

HIM "Come on!"

I look around to make sure no one's within earshot. He leans forward.

ME "Okay, but it'll involve a lot of work."

HIM "I can do it."

ME "How are you with building things?"

HIM "I'm okay."

ME "Okay. First, we have to find blueprints for a time machine."

HIM "Oh, man."

CHRISTMAS MUSIC

GRADE TEN STUDENT "Sir, can we change the music on your stereo?"

ME "You guys asked me to play Christmas music while you worked."

HER "Yeah, but this music kind of sucks."

ME "This is my Bing Crosby and Elvis mix."

HER "Do you have any idea how young we are?"

ME "That's a very nice way of pointing out how old I am."

HER "Exactly."

ME "Fine."

STICKY SITUATION

GRADE NINE STUDENT "Sir, there's gum under my desk!"

ME "Is it new or old?"

HER "I'm not going to touch it."

ME "Well, if you don't figure out if it's hardened or soft, I can't help you."

She reaches hesitantly under her desk.

HER "Ew! It's solid!"

ME "Oh, that means it's old. It's like part of the desk now, so don't worry about it."

HER "You're no help!"

ME "I believe in empowering you."

SPANKED

GRADE EIGHT STUDENT "Sir, what's spanking the monkey?"

ME "Where did you hear that term?"

HIM "I heard my dad say it to his friends, and they were laughing."

ME "You should ask your father what it means."

HIM "Why can't you just tell me?"

ME "It'll be better if your father explains it."

HIM "Okay, but I just want to know why hitting a monkey is funny to people. That's mean."

ME "Make sure you say that to your dad, too."

EASY LIKE MONDAY MORNING

During a test in English 10, one of my students is tapping his pencil very loudly, distracting his peers. I walk over to his desk so that I can whisper to him.

ME "Hey, do you mind not doing that?"

He looks around. His classmates are shooting him dirty looks.

HIM "Why's everyone is such a pissy mood?"
ME "You know, some people find tests stressful. And you drumming on your desk is not helping them concentrate."
HIM "Then they all should have prepared like me. This test is easy."

There are groans of protest from some students. Some comments are not so nice. He's smiling, rolling with it.

I quickly scan his test answers. Half of them are wrong.

ME "Um, did you really study?"
HIM "*Writing* the test is easy. Doing well is a different story. Either way, why stress?"
ME "You worry me sometimes."

SIMPLE QUESTION

A grade eight student approaches my desk, textbook in hand.

HIM "Sir, you're an Asian, right?"

That is all.

DID SHE STUTTER?

One of my grade ten students beckons me over to his desk near the end of class. He's trying to settle a debate with his friends. He holds his cellphone up to me, showing me a text conversation between him and a girl.

HIM "Sir, how do you interpret that?"
ME "She's not interested in you."

His friends start laughing.

HIM "How do you know? Like, how are you so sure?"
ME "Right there, she says she's not interested."
HIM "She's playing."
ME "Did she stutter?"

He looks at his phone.

HIM "How am I supposed to know that?"

MIRRORING

GRADE TEN STUDENT "Sir, why are there so many songs about the weather? You ever think of that?"
ME "That's a good question. Why do you think songwriters look to the weather for inspiration?"
HIM "I just asked you that."

THREE'S COMPANY

GRADE ELEVEN STUDENT "Sir, what was your favourite TV show growing up?"

ME "Gosh, there were so many. When I was a kid I really liked *Three's Company*."

HIM "What was that about?"

ME "It was a sitcom about a guy who lived with two women."

HIM (Smirking) "Oh yeah!"

ME "It wasn't like that. It was about friendship and respect."

HIM "Bo-ring!"

WHITE CHRISTMAS

GRADE NINE STUDENT "Sir, when did you stop believing in Santa Claus?"

ME "I don't think I ever really believed he was real."

HER "You never did? Why?"

ME "Well, Santa was always white on television, but at my parents' church, Santa was Korean and wore a fake beard and was my father's friend. And his Korean accent really threw the whole illusion off. His 'Merry Christmas' sounded like 'Meh-dee Chdismas.'"

HER "That's so sad you didn't have a white Santa like everyone else!"

A MILE IN HIS SHOES

One of my grade nine students is missing a shoelace and has asked me if I have an extra one.

ME "Are you walking home?"

HIM "Yup."

ME "Here. I'm driving, so I don't have to walk far. Why don't you use one of my laces?"

I start to unlace one of my boots.

HIM "That's okay."
ME "Don't worry. I'll be fine."
HIM "No, I mean—"

He looks embarrassed by his thoughts.
I look down at my boots.

ME "Is it because they don't match your shoes?"
HIM "Yeah, it'd be kind of weird."

AMBIDEXTROUS

GRADE TEN STUDENT "Sir, what's that word for when you're good at using both your hands?"
ME "Ambidextrous."
HIM "No, that's not it."
ME "Sorry, I don't know any other words for that."
HIM "I know it. It's just on the tip of my tongue."
ME "You sure it's not ambidextrous?"
HIM "How do you spell that?"

I spell it out for him.

HIM "No. That's not it."
ME "So, you want a word describing how someone can use both left and right hands equally well?"

HIM "Yeah. But it doesn't have to be equal. Like, when athletes move well."

I sit thinking for a while.

ME "Coordinated?"
HIM "That's it."

And this is why I keep a bottle of ibuprofen in my desk.

SELF—IMPROVEMENT

GRADE NINE STUDENT "Sir, these lights suck. It's time for a change."

I look up at our old fluorescent lights built into the ceiling.

ME "I agree. But it'll be a while before our district has the money to change all that."
HER "Why don't we do a fundraiser to switch it ourselves?"
ME "I don't think we'd be allowed to switch only our room lights. It'd have to be schoolwide."
HER "Not every teacher's room is the same."
ME "I know, but the structures have to be."
HER "I don't think so. Like, Mr Smith has these great posters all over his walls, and you have nothing. And Mrs Kelly has nice decorations and colours, and your room's really boring."
ME "Thank you for letting me know how inferior my room is."
HER "You have to know your faults so you can improve on them."

RESOLUTIONS

GRADE TEN STUDENT "Sir, any New Year's resolutions this year?"

ME "Not really."

HER "Not even to get in shape or anything?"

ME "What are you trying to tell me?"

HER "Oh. Nothing. Sorry."

ME "What's your resolution? To avoid insulting people by accident?"

HER "How'd you know?"

AULDER LANG SYNE

GRADE TWELVE STUDENT "Sir, what did you do for New Year's?"

ME "Just had a few friends over."

HIM "Did your friends trash your place?"

ME "Do you have any idea what a forty-year-old's life looks like?"

HOOKING ME UP

After five frustrating minutes trying to hook up the video projector to my laptop in my English 11 class ...

STUDENT "Sir, you need help?"

ME "Sure."

HIM (To the rest of the class) "Anyone know how to hook this thing up?"

ONE SMALL STEP FOR MAN

GRADE TWELVE STUDENT "Sir, wouldn't it be cool if we sent people to the moon?"

Kids start laughing.

HIM (To class) "Shut up! It'd be cool."

ME "You mean again?"

HIM (Kind of getting it) "No way."

I motion him towards my computer and cue up a YouTube video titled "Moon Landing 1969." He watches, his eyes growing big as it plays.

HIM (Pointing at the screen) "When was this???"

I move his finger about five inches closer to the screen so that he's now pointing at the date.

HIM (Laughing at me) "Nineteen sixty-nine! How was I supposed to know that? I wasn't even born then."

NEVER FRIENDED

GRADE NINE STUDENT "Sir, I found you on Facebook."

ME "Good for you."

HER "Why haven't you added me yet?"

ME "You know my rule: not until you've graduated."

HER "That's just weird."

ME "What's weirder: the teacher who doesn't want to be friends with his students or the student who wants to be friends with her teacher?"

HER "I don't want to be friends. I just want to look at pictures of your dogs."

ME "Oh, well, that's not weird at all."

MEAT AND KIMCHI

GRADE EIGHT STUDENT "Sir, do you eat kimchi every day?"

ME "Why? Because I'm Korean?"

HIM "Yeah."

ME "You're Irish. Do you eat potatoes every day?"

HIM "Almost, yeah. I love french fries!"

ME "Well ... then ... no, I don't."

TASTE IT

GRADE TWELVE STUDENT "Sir, Skittles?"

ME "No thanks."

HIM "You don't like Skittles?"

ME "Just not right now."

HIM "C'mon, sir, taste the rainbow."

His classmates giggle. I relent, holding open my palm as he drops three candies into my hand.

ME "Three? That's hardly a rainbow."

HIM "It's just a saying."

PROBABLY SOME YOUNG GUY

Grade nine student invites me to his father's Indian restaurant. I look it up online.

ME "Wow. It's got a ninety-one-percent approval rating on Urbanspoon."

HIM "What does that mean?"

ME "Well, if ten people went to eat there, nine of them loved it and one person didn't."

HIM "Probably some Chinese guy."

BOOK CHAT

GRADE TWELVE STUDENT "Sir, what's your favourite novel?"

ME "Do you want to know the one I enjoyed the most or the one that meant the most to me?"

HIM "Never mind. I only have a few minutes."

AHNOLD

GRADE NINE STUDENT "Sir, have you seen *Total Recall*?"

ME "The remake or the original?"

HIM "There was an original?"

ME "Of course. With Ahnold."

The student's face doesn't register any recognition.

ME (In a thick Schwarzenegger accent) "I'll be back."

He's never heard that.

ME "It's not a tumour!"

Nothing.

ME "*Hasta la vista*, baby!"

HIM "Is this all from the original?"

ME "Never mind."

SHOWER, BATH AND BEYOND

GRADE ELEVEN STUDENT "Sir, do you take showers or baths?"

ME "Showers. Why?"

HIM "Nothing. Just wondering why no one takes baths anymore."

ME "I take it you're a shower man?"

HIM "I'd rather not say. It's kind of personal. You know?"

ME "Right. Sorry for intruding."

PRINCELY

GRADE TEN STUDENT "Sir, what did you do this weekend?"

ME "I went to the Prince concert."

HIM "Is that the guy with the spoons?"

ME "Yeah ... what?"

CPR

GRADE EIGHT STUDENT "Sir, how do you spell CPR?"

ME "How do you think?"

HIM "C?"

I nod.

HIM "P?"

I nod again.

HIM "I'll take it from here."

HER FAVE

I ask grade nine students to name their favourite band or singer.

ME "Um, you were supposed to describe your favourite musical artist."

HER "I did."

ME "You wrote that your favourite singer ... is you."

HER "Yeah. I love listening to the sound of my own voice."

ME "Yes. But I already know that."

HOME SWEET HOME

GRADE TWELVE STUDENT "Sir, I need your digits."

ME "Why?"

HIM "For homework questions."

ME "You have my work email for that."

HIM "What if I have questions in the middle of the night? You never check your email from home."

ME "Exactly."

1999

GRADE ELEVEN STUDENT "Happy New Year, sir."

ME "Thank you. How was your New Year's?"

HIM "Man, we partied like it was 1999."

ME "I'm surprised anyone your age knows Prince."

HIM "Prince who?"

THE CONVERSATIONALIST

GRADE TWELVE STUDENT "Sir, I saw you in the mall last weekend."

ME "Yeah?"

HIM "Yeah. What were you doing there?"

ME "Shopping perhaps?"

HIM "Nice."

ME "Great talking with you."

HIM "Cool."

STUPID

GRADE NINE STUDENT "Sir, my dad let me taste champagne on New Year's."

ME "Did you like it?"

HER "It was gross. Why do adults drink it?"

ME "They like the way it makes them feel."

HER "It made me want to puke."

ME "It has that effect on lots of adults, too."

HER "And it makes them stupid."

ME "You're right there, too."

HER "I hope I'm never that stupid that I drink something gross just to become stupider."

ME "I don't think you'll ever be that stupid."

VEGANS

GRADE NINE STUDENT "Sir, what's the difference between vegans and vegetarians?"

ME "From what I understand, vegetarians don't eat meat, but vegans will avoid using all animal products including milk and eggs."

HIM "I guess I'm not either of them, then."

ME "How is that?"

HIM "I eat fish and sometimes burgers."

ME "Yeah, you're not even close."

IN THE RAIN

GRADE TWELVE STUDENT "Sir, how do you stand living here? It rains so much."

ME "I don't mind the rain. It's got a certain romance to it."

HIM "I like how you roll, sir."

ME "I don't make out in the rain."

HIM "Oh. Never mind, then."

EXCUSE

A grade ten student walks into class fifteen minutes late.

HIM "Sorry I'm late, sir."

ME "Don't worry about it. Just make up the time after school with me."

HIM "But I have a good excuse."

ME "You slept in?"

HIM "But for a good reason."

ME "Let's hear it."

HIM "Really?"

ME "Yeah."

HIM "My alarm wasn't working."

ME "That's the best you could come up with?"

HIM "You put me on the spot."

A GEM

I have been away for a day and return to find that the substitute teacher sent one of my best grade eleven students to the office.

ME "What got into you?"

HIM "Sir, you had to be here. She was crazy."

The other students are nodding.

ME "In what way?"

HIM "She was talking about her gemstones or something and how rocks have spirits."

The students back him up.

ME "So what did you say?"

HIM "I told her that her ideas were ridiculous. You would have been disappointed if I didn't."

ME "Regardless of her ideas, she's a guest in our house."

HIM "Well, sir, stop inviting crazy ladies into our house."

GRAND RACISM

An argument breaks out at the back of the class. A black student and his Asian friend are in each other's faces.

ME (Separating them) "What the hell is going on here?"

STUDENT 1 "He says I should be better at *Grand Theft Auto* because I should be used to running from the cops."

ME (To Student 2) "Really? You said that?"

STUDENT 2 "Yeah. But he said I shouldn't drive cuz I'm Chinese!"

I look at Student 1.

STUDENT 1 "I guess it went both ways."

READING

GRADE TEN STUDENT "Sir, what do you do at night? Watch TV?"

ME "I like to spend time reading."

HIM "What do you read?"

ME "Anything that'll blow my mind."

HIM "Man, you need to learn to relax."

NO PROBLEM

A grade twelve student places her marked essay on my desk in front of me.

HER "Sir, why did you circle this part?"

ME "That's a run-on sentence. You should break it up with a semicolon or dash if you're going to keep it as one sentence."

HER "Why can E.E. Cummings get away with doing whatever he wants with punctuation and the rest of us can't?"

ME "If you start writing like Cummings, I'll never correct your punctuation again."

HER "Deal!"

RAP

GRADE TEN STUDENT "Sir, do you know how to rap?"

ME "No."

HIM "How come?"

ME "Probably the area I grew up in."

HIM "Where was that?"

ME "Well, in west Philadelphia, born and raised, on the playground was where I spent most of my days."

HIM "Hey, that rhymed!"

AQUEDUCT

During a review of the Roman Empire during Social Studies 9 ...

ME "Does anyone remember what an aqueduct is?"
STUDENT 1 "It's a duck that goes on water."
STUDENT 2 "All ducks go on water! Use your head."

I write *aqueduct* on the board.

STUDENT 2 "It's waterproof tape."

A REMINDER THAT I'M ASIAN

A grade eleven student walks into my classroom ten minutes after the bell.

ME "Why are you so late?"
HER "There was a major car accident on the way to school."
ME "Okay. Have a seat."
HER "There are some seriously bad drivers out there. No offence, sir."

KID MD

GRADE EIGHT STUDENT "Sir, where were you yesterday?"
ME "I was sick."
HER "What'd you have?"
ME "I don't know. Just didn't feel well."
HER "What were your symptoms?"
ME "I felt sick."
HER "Hmm. I'd say you had a cold."

ARCHIE HERE

GRADE TWELVE STUDENT "Sir, growing up, were you into Betty
    or Veronica?"

ME "Veronica. I would always be attracted to Veronicas."

HIM "Why's that?"

ME "I'm not sure."

HIM "Did your mother withhold her affections?"

ME "Mr Saunders start psychology with you?"

HIM "This morning."

IT'S ALL IN THE DELIVERY

One of my jokes has just died a shameful death in my English 11
class.

ME "Really? No one? Okay, then."

STUDENT "I think it was your delivery, sir."

ME "What was wrong with my delivery?"

HER "You delivered that joke."

Her joke gets a rapturous reception.

ME "Take a bow."

She does, beaming.

SPEECHLESS EVER AFTER

A grade nine student has made me oven mitts as a gift.

ME "Wow, thanks! But what made you think I bake?"

HIM "I figured either you or your wife does."

ME "What makes you think I'm married?"

HIM "Because you're always happy."

ME "And happy people are married?"

HIM "Yeah. Cuz my mom's always really sad and she's not married anymore."

ME "Oh."

PUSH-UPS

One of my grade nine students hasn't finished his homework.

HIM "How many push-ups would you like me to do, sir?"

ME "None. I'd rather you just did the homework."

HIM "I'll make it up to you."

He goes into push-up position on the floor.

HIM "How many?"

ME "Do what you want."

He starts doing push-ups. His peers are laughing. I sit at my desk and wait.

He stops after twenty.

HIM "There."

ME "There what?"

HIM "We're even."

ME "How's that even? You still owe me your homework."

HIM "Yeah, but don't you feel a little bit guilty now? A little bit?"

ME "It's like you don't know me at all."

MR BAE

GRADE NINE STUDENT "Sir, do you know what your name means?"

ME "Yes."

HER "Does your girlfriend call you bae Bae?"

ME "No. She calls me by my first name."

HER "She calls you bae Paul?"

She laughs.

ME "No. Just Paul."

HER "Doesn't anyone call you bae?"

ME "Just you guys."

HER "Gross!"

POST-ADOLESCENCE

GRADE TWELVE STUDENT "Sir, what is *that* on your forehead?"

ME "Um, it's called a pimple and thanks for pointing it out in the middle of class."

HER "Oh, sorry. But you're in your forties. How do you still get zits?"

ME "Stress, from students like you."

JUICE

GRADE EIGHT STUDENT "Sir, do you drink a lot of juice?"

ME "No. Why?"

HIM "I don't know. You just seem like you would."

Some students are as befuddled as me and start giggling.

ME "What is it about me that makes you think that?"

HIM "You just look like you would enjoy a good juice."

ME "Who doesn't?"

HIM "See?"

ME "Does anyone else know what's going on here?"

FACEBOOK

GRADE TWELVE STUDENT "Sir, are you Facebook friends with your parents?"

ME "No."

HER "Why not?"

ME "My mother asked me how to make an account and I told her there's a monthly fee. So she didn't join."

HER "That's mean!"

STUDENT 2 "That's brilliant!"

HER "This is why I never want sons."

BEDTIME STORIES

One of my grade nine students is upset because I told her mother that she frequently breaks classroom rules by texting in class.

HER "I hope you're happy! She said she's going to confiscate my phone every night for a month now."

ME "That sucks."

HER "I can't believe you actually told her."

ME "But I warned you twice I was going to phone her if you continued."

HER "I didn't think you'd actually do it. What am I supposed to do now?"

ME "What do you mean? You have your phone now."

HER "At night. What am I supposed to do at night?"

ME "Oh, I don't know. Sleep?"

HER "I can't sleep unless I read."

ME "Then read."

HER "How? I told you she takes my phone at night."

ME "Right."

GIRL ADVICE

GRADE NINE STUDENT "Sir, sometimes I wish you were a girl."

ME "Why?"

HER "Because you're good at giving guy advice. If you were a girl, you could give us girl advice."

ME "What are you talking about? You ask me for advice all the time."

HER "But it's not the same."

ME "How's that?"

HER "Because you were never a girl so don't know everything about being a girl."

ME "You asked me what I thought of your fingernail art last month and I gave you pretty good advice then."

HER "No you didn't. You said the same thing my dad said. That's not helpful."

ME "What did I say, again?"

HER "You told me to stay within the lines. And then you laughed."

ME "Your dad's pretty funny."

ORIENTALISM

One of my Chinese students approaches me during English 10.

HIM "Sir, why are we 'Asian' and not 'Oriental'?"

ME "'Oriental' is considered politically incorrect now and kind of offensive."

HIM "Why's that?"

ME "It's a term used by white colonialists to describe a huge group of people."

HIM "But, isn't 'Asian' also a term given to us by white people? Like, anything we call ourselves in English is probably not something we came up with ourselves, right?"

ME "Your brain has outgrown me."

TOO SWEET

A grade ten student is eating a bag of candies during class.

ME   "You shouldn't eat so much sugar."

HER "Why?"

ME   "Did you know diabetes is one of the leading causes of death in the United States?"

HER "Well, this is Canada, not the States."

ME   "You're right. Sugar works way differently up here."

TEST PREPARATION

In English 11, handing out tests.

ME "Please keep your tests face down. You may start when I tell you to."

STUDENT "What if we don't want to?"

ME "If you don't want to what? Start?"

HIM "Yeah."

ME "That's completely up to you."

HIM "Cool. I won't be ready for another five minutes or something."

ME "We'll be here for you if you need us."

MO' PROBLEMS

During English 10, a normally talkative boy is quiet all class.

ME "You okay?"

HIM "Yup."

ME "Girlfriend problems?"

HIM (Looks around to make sure no one's listening) "Yup."

ME "What's the problem?"

HIM "I want a different girlfriend."

ME "Gotcha."

ANXIETY

In English 11, on the topic of anxiety ...

ME "Anxiety can also be caused by positive experiences. For instance, I remember when I was your age I really liked this new girl at school. I couldn't sleep all night just thinking about her."

STUDENT "You know what you should have done?"

ME "Whatever you're about to say, I'm going to repeat to your mother at the next parent-teacher night."

HIM "Never mind, then."

HAMARTIA

ME "So, what is Macbeth's fatal flaw?"

STUDENT "His woman."

ME "Maybe you could elaborate?"

HIM "He's whipped."

ME "What do you mean by that, in case there are some who don't know what that means?"

HIM "It means he has to grow a pair."

ME "A pair."

HIM "You know, a pair of—"

ME "Yeah, we got it now."

WE DON'T NEED ANOTHER HERO

I have just assigned a project in which the students write about someone they consider a hero, living or dead.

STUDENT "Sir, can we write about you?"

ME (Flattered) "Me? Why do you consider me your hero?"

HIM "Cuz you're marking it."

DRUGS

A grade twelve student hands me a doctor's note.

ME "What does this mean?"

HIM (Giddily) "I'm going to miss three weeks of school cuz of knee surgery."

ME "You going to be drugged up the whole time?"

HIM "No, but I won't be able to walk."

ME "That's fine. I'll deliver your work to your house for you. I'll make arrangements with your mom."

HIM "No! I'll be on drugs. I'll be on drugs!"

ME "Too late."

HIM "Man, I'm never saying *no* to drugs again."

JUSTIN BIEBER

ME "Did you hear that Justin Bieber is going to host *Saturday Night Live*?"

HER "Yeah. Everyone knows. Stop trying to pretend you're cool, sir."

ME "Yeah, I'm trying to pretend I'm cool by pretending I like Justin Bieber."

BLACK HISTORY MONTH

During a Black History Month lesson for grade nines I show them signs from the American South in the 1950s, with *No negroes or apes allowed* written on one.

ME "It's like in that Bruce Lee movie where he kicks that sign that says *No dogs and Chinese allowed*. Why was that sign up?"

STUDENT (Serious) "Oh, cuz Chinese eat dogs."

IN THE DUMPS

GRADE TEN STUDENT "Sir, have you ever been dumped by a girl?"
ME (Jokingly) "Of course not."

He looks down at his desk.

ME "I'm kidding. Of course I've been dumped. I've been dumped lots of times."

His face brightens up.

ME "So, you were just dumped recently?"
HIM "No. But, man, that's sad! How did you take it?"
ME "How did this become about me?"

WEEKENDS

STUDENT "How was your weekend, Sir?"
ME "Good. Could have used more sleep."
HER "Is that why you have those huge bags under your eyes?"
ME "Get out."

HARLEM SHAKE

GRADE NINE STUDENT "Sir, we're taping a Harlem Shake video after school. Can you come out and be a part of it?"
ME "I don't know. I'm still waiting for the Shamrock Shake to come back."
HER (Blank stare)
ME "I'll be there."

VALENTINE'S DAY

GRADE TWELVE STUDENT "Sir, are you getting your girlfriend flowers
for Valentine's Day?"

ME "No."

HER "Why not?"

ME "Because I don't like what flowers represent. They bloom
and die very quickly, and I don't want our relationship to be like
that."

The boys look impressed.

HER "You expect her to buy that bullshit?"

GREETINGS

GRADE ELEVEN STUDENT "Hi, sir. How are you doing?"

ME "I'm doing well, thank you."

HIM "And your dogs?"

ME "They're well."

HIM "And your girlfriend?"

ME "She's well."

He's thinking.

ME "I've got parents."

HIM "How are they?"

ME "Good."

He's thinking again.

ME "That's about it."

HIM "Great."

ACADEMY AWARDS

GRADE TWELVE STUDENT "Sir, did you watch the Academy Awards?"

ME "No. I don't think you should make a contest of art."

HIM "Why not?"

ME "It's so subjective."

HIM "But you gave me a C-minus on my last essay. That's grading my art!"

ME "Your essay was about why donuts are better than bagels."

HIM "What if they made it into a movie?"

THE BACHELOR

GRADE TWELVE STUDENT "Sir, you ever think about going on *The Bachelor*?"

ME "No. I don't think my girlfriend would like it."

HIM "But think how much fun it'd be with all those women."

ME "I never thought of it that way. Let me clear it with her and I'll get back to you."

HIM "Cool."

I stare at him.

HIM "Oh. You're kidding."

HIS CYRANO

GRADE ELEVEN STUDENT "Sir, how do you write a love letter?"

ME "Ah, you want me to be your Cyrano?"

HIM "My what?"

ME "Cyrano de Bergerac. A French writer who was immortalized in a play in the late nineteenth century. He was known as—"

HIM "Do I Facebook or email her?"

ME "Either."

HIM "Thanks."

THE WORST–LAID PLANS OF MICE AND GRADE EIGHTS

I heard from one of my nicer students in grade eight English class that while I was absent the day before, a few of the boys ground up some chalk and mixed it into the substitute teacher's coffee. I walk into class with a furrowed brow, deep in thought.

STUDENT 1 "Sir, welcome back. Something wrong?"

ME "Oh, it's nothing to concern you. It's about my substitute teacher."

STUDENT 1 "What about him?"

ME "I got a message just now from the office saying he had to be rushed to the hospital yesterday after work due to some abdominal pains."

STUDENT 2 "What?"

Student 2 shoots Student 1 an angry glare. Student 1 looks very guilty.

ME "Yeah. Strange how everything's going great one minute, and the next thing you know, you're off getting your stomach pumped. He must have eaten something bad. I hope he's all right."

Student 1's eyes start to well up.

STUDENT 1 "Sir, there's something we have to tell you."

ME "Yes?"

STUDENT 1 "It's my fault. I did a prank on him."

STUDENT 2 "Me, too. I helped him do it."

ME "Do what?"

STUDENT 1 "We took some chalk and put it in his coffee."

STUDENT 2 "We thought it'd be funny."

ME "Is it funny?"

Both boys shake their heads despairingly.

ME "You know what's funny?"

They look up.

ME "The looks on your faces when you find out I lied. The teacher's fine. But you're both in a lot of trouble."

They both look immensely relieved.

STUDENT 2 "I've never been so happy about getting in trouble."

THE FUNDAMENTALS OF NAME-CALLING

I'm breaking up a scuffle in English 9 between a boy and two girls.

ME "What's going on here?"

GIRL 1 "He called me a terrorist."

ME "You did?"

HIM "I meant to say fundamentalist."

ME "Why would you say that?"

HIM "She called me stupid."

ME "And why are you involved?"

GIRL 2 "He called me a slut."

ME "Why in the world would you call someone that?"

HIM "Look at the way she's dressed!"

ME "And you're calling *her* a fundamentalist?"

LOVE MARKETING

During a discussion about the school's upcoming Valentine's Day dance ...

GRADE TWELVE STUDENT "Sir, there's too much consumer pressure surrounding Valentine's."

ME "How's that?"

HIM "Well, if you have a girlfriend and you're totally devoted to her, but you forget to buy her a gift on that one day, suddenly she takes that small slip to mean that you don't love her."

ME "You forgot to get her a gift, didn't you?"

HIM "It's been a busy month."

CAST

A grade eight student walks into class wearing a cast on his arm.

ME "How'd you do that?"

HIM "I broke it."

ME "I can see that. How'd it happen?"

HIM "I fell."

ME "While doing what?"

HIM "Walking."

ME "Feel free to predict my next questions whenever you want."

BOYS CAN BE AWFUL

GRADE EIGHT GIRL "Sir, did you know boys can be really mean?"

ME "Of course I do. I'm a teacher."

She's looking down at her hands.

ME "Did one of them say something to you today?"

HER "Someone said my face is weird."

ME "Was it Brian?"

HER "How did you know?"

ME "Because Brian's got awful taste. Look at the way he spikes his hair."

She giggles.

ME "If he had good taste, I'd be a bit worried. But are you going to listen to a guy with that hair? C'mon!"

THE FIRST POEM

GRADE ELEVEN STUDENT "Sir, the first person to ever write a poem—what do you think the poem was about?"

ME "That's a good question. I have no clue."

HIM "I bet it was a love poem from a guy."

ME "What makes you think that?"

HIM "Because guys put a lot of thought into new ways to get girls."

CUE LAUGH TRACK

It's lunchtime and I'm playing some Bon Jovi on the stereo, and a grade nine student walks in.

HER "Sir, every time I come here while you're playing your music, it makes me feel like I'm walking into an old eighties sitcom."

ME "How do you know what the eighties were like?"

HER "It feels corny."

ME "It's like you were there."

SEXY IS SUBJECTIVE

GRADE ELEVEN STUDENT "Sir, who do you find sexy?"

ME "That's easy. Cary Grant. Or young Robert Redford."

She looks puzzled. So do her friends.

ME "You probably want one closer to your generation. Johnny Depp? Though I've always found Matt Damon's confidence alluring."

HER "I mean women."

ME "Oh. My girlfriend, definitely."

LILAC WINE

While introducing a poetry project to my English 12 class, I play Jeff Buckley's "Lilac Wine" and we parse the lyrics. Most of the students love it, but some are unmoved.

GRADE TWELVE STUDENT "So what's the big deal? There's lots of songs about getting your heart broken."

ME "You don't hear the pain and longing in his voice? You don't hear him falter at the line 'because it brings me back you'? You don't buy it?"

HIM "If she's gone, I say, 'Next!'"

Several girls roll their eyes. I start laughing.

HIM "You don't believe me?"

ME "No, I do. It's just that I never knew you were so scared of stuff."

HIM "Just cuz I don't like wimpy love songs?"

ME "It takes great courage to open yourself to things that may end up hurting you, like love. Great courage. To deny it is playing it safe. But the life you want is totally up to you."

HIM "You're not gonna make me like that song."

THERE'S A WORD FOR THAT

GRADE ELEVEN STUDENT "Sir, what in the world is this word?"

ME "That's schadenfreude. It's German for deriving pleasure from another's misfortune."

HER "Don't we have an English word for that?"

ME "Not really."

HER "How about being a bitch?"

ME "That's more than one word."

HER "Oh yeah."

LOVE SONGS

During a discussion about love songs and poetry in English 12 ...

GRADE TWELVE STUDENT "Sir, has a song ever made you cry?"

ME "Yes. The last time was in 1997. I had just gotten divorced. I was a mess. Didn't have anyone to turn to who would understand me. I'd never been hurt like that before. So I got into my car one day and started driving south. Next thing I knew, I was driving down the California coast. It was beautiful, but I was broken.

And then the Verve came on the CD player. The song "One Day." I knew the song well but had never really paid attention to the lyrics. The music started, and very gently, Richard Ashcroft hit this opening line: 'One day maybe we will dance again, under fiery skies; one day maybe you will love again, love that never dies.'

I tell you, it sounded like a close friend telling me that. And I wept. I was crying so much I had to pull the car over. And I started laughing because it was all so ridiculous and pathetic and beautiful. And I knew then that despite the pain, everything was going to be all right."

The class is silent. Everyone looks like they're a bit in shock.

ME "Anyway, back to our subject?"

HIM "Can you play the song?"

ME "Maybe after we've done some poetry."

HIM "This *is* poetry."

A CORNER

Five minutes into an assignment in English 9, I notice one student hasn't even started and is just staring off into space.

ME "Is there a problem?"

HER "I don't have a pen."

ME "Why didn't you just ask me for one?"

HER "You told me last week that if I forgot my pen one more time that I was going to have a detention."

ME "So you thought just sitting there would be an acceptable solution?"

HER "You kind of forced me into this choice."

THE CATCHER IN THE RYE

GRADE ELEVEN STUDENT "Sir, can I switch books?"

ME "You don't like the one we're reading?"

HIM "I'm just not into it."

ME "Why's that?"

HIM "Holden's a bit of a whiner. I'm already sick of him."

ME "I've always thought of him as disaffected the way a lot of teenagers are."

HIM "I've got three exams next week and I work weekends. I don't have time to be disaffected."

CARELESS MUTTERINGS

GRADE TEN STUDENT "Sir, what's a nice way to break up with someone?"

ME "There is none. Just be straightforward and tell them."

HIM "How have you done it in the past?"

ME "Well, one time I told this girl that I was never gonna dance again, cuz guilty feet have got no rhythm. Though it's easy to pretend, I know you're not a fool."

HIM (Taking out a pen and opening his notebook) "Can you repeat that?"

SOMEWHERE I HAVE NEVER TRAVELLED

ME "What is the poet trying to evoke with the line 'Nobody, not even the rain, has such small hands'?"

GRADE TWELVE STUDENT "You know what they say about raindrops with small hands?"

ME "Don't."

HIM "All right."

UNSANITARY

I've just handed out a set of novels to my English 10 class.

STUDENT "Sir, do you have any newer copies?"

ME "No. Just those."

HER "It's a bit unsanitary, don't you think? Like, who knows how many kids wiped their noses and then flipped through these pages?"

ME "I never thought about that. Man, imagine what the bottom of your desk must be like."

HER "Oh God!"

OLD RIDE

I'm driving some of my grade nine rugby players to a game.

STUDENT "Sir, are you serious?"

He's pointing at my cassette player in the dashboard.

ME "Yup."

He's laughing.

HIM "Who has a cassette player in his car still?"

I slow the car down.

ME "The guy not taking the bus."
HIM "Oh. I take it back, then."

BIG PLANS

GRADE ELEVEN STUDENT "Big plans for the weekend, sir?"
ME "Of course. Going to cook up a big dinner, then go on a big hike. How about you? Big plans?"
HIM "If you think your plans are big, mine are humongous."
ME "Why do I keep answering you?"

OSCARS 2011

GRADE TWELVE STUDENT "Sir, did you watch the Oscars?"
ME "No. I don't really enjoy contests of art."
HER "It's not about art really. It's about Hollywood."
ME "That's pretty good."
HER "I just made that up. I should get an Oscar for that."

PULL MY FINGER

One of my grade eight students approaches me in my classroom during lunch. His friends are giggling behind him.

HIM "Sir, pull my finger."

ME "What is this? The seventies? No way."

HIM "It's not what you think."

ME "What do you think I think it is?"

HIM "Huh?"

ME "What do you think I'm guessing it is?"

HIM "Why won't you pull it?"

ME "Are you serious?"

HIM "It's not what you think!"

ME "Okay, but if it's—"

He farts.

HIM "You were too slow!"

ME "Open a window before you leave."

A TWENTY

GRADE TEN STUDENT "Sir, can you break a twenty?"

He holds out a twenty dollar bill.

ME "Sorry. I don't have any cash on me."

HIM "Too bad. I was gonna buy you a coffee."

ME "Well, that's nice of you."

He stands there looking at me, waiting.

HIM "Oh, so you really don't have change."

ME "You thought I was lying?"

HIM "I thought maybe you were being cheap."

ME "But we were just going to exchange twenty dollars for twenty dollars."

HIM "I'm not good at math."

BELLY SHAMING

GRADE TEN STUDENT "Sir, your belly's sticking out."

ME "I'm in my forties. My belly's supposed to stick out."

HER "Maybe this is why you always have back problems."

ME "Can we not talk about my back?"

HER "Does it make you uncomfortable?"

ME "Talking about the state of my body with one of my students? Yes, it does."

HER "You shouldn't be ashamed of your body."

ME "I wasn't, until you pointed out my belly."

HER "Then you should do something about it. It's not healthy."

MY CUP RUNNETH OVER

GRADE NINE STUDENT "Sir, do you have an extra cup I could use?"

ME "Sure."

I hand her one of my extra coffee mugs. She looks it over distastefully.

ME "Is there a problem?"

HER "It's kind of brown on the inside."

ME "Those are just coffee stains. It's been through the dishwasher. It's clean."

HER "Then why's it so brown?"

ME "Cups stain. That's just the way it is."

HER "Why do you say it's 'just the way it is' instead of 'I don't know'?"

ME "Is this still about you wanting to borrow a cup?"

DANCE WORLD

GRADE TWELVE STUDENT "Sir, did you have gangs back in your day?"

ME "Not at my school. It sounds weird, but back in the mid-eighties, rivals crews would meet up and instead of fight, we'd have breakdance battles."

HIM "It sounds like a movie. That was for real?"

ME "Yeah, it was a weird time."

HIM "Wait, so who judged who won?"

ME "It would almost always be obvious. You knew when someone was a better dancer than you."

HIM "I wish it was like that today. If that happened now, if someone beat someone dancing, they'd probably get beat up or shot."

ME "Yeah, there seemed to be a tiny window of a few years in the eighties when everything felt really safe. It was all about the dance."

HIM "It's like you grew up in a musical."

BRANDED

GRADE TEN STUDENT "Sir, why do they make us wear the same
   gym strip?"

ME "It's a safety issue. Our school's so large that we need a way to
   know who goes to our school and who's an intruder."

HIM "Oh. So it's not to protect us from corporate symbols like Nike
   and Adidas?"

ME "If that were the case, all your running shoes would be
   banned."

HIM "That's true. I don't think I could even name a no-name brand
   of runners."

NOT EVEN THE RAIN

At the end of an English 10 lesson on poetry, a student approaches
my desk.

HIM "Sir, that was a cool lesson. I don't think I'll ever look at the
   rain the same way."

ME "That's what good poetry does."

HIM "I don't even know what it means when he says the rain has
   small hands, but it makes sense for some reason."

ME "I know what you mean."

HIM "You sometimes think of raindrops as tiny little people jumping
   to their deaths, too?"

ME "Sorry. I *thought* I knew what you meant."

GRADE ELEVEN STUDENT "Sir, I found your blog."

ME "Oh."

HER "Don't worry. I won't tell anyone."

ME "Thanks."

HER "Have you written about me yet?"

ME "Of course."

HER "Really? Which story?"

I take her to the computer and go to the story.

HER "I didn't say that!"

ME "No, you're the other one. I changed you to a grade ten boy."

HER "Wow. Well, now he looks like a genius."

MUST BE QUITE THE LIFE

A student in English 9 calls me to her desk.

HER "Sir, would you like to read my autobiography?"

She hands me a thick journal.

ME "You sure you want to give me that? You don't want to keep it to yourself, given all the secrets that might be in there?"

HER "It reads more like a thriller."

ME "Your autobiography?"

HER "I've been told it's quite harrowing."

And that was the first and only time a student used the word "harrowing" in my classroom.

TRUE HEARTBREAK

GRADE TWELVE STUDENT "Sir, how many times have you had your heart broken?"

ME "Several times. I can't even count them all."

HER "Really?"

ME "Yeah. But I'm not the only Canucks fan who feels that way."

HER (Angry stare)

ME "It's an old sports joke."

HER "The girls usually left you?"

ME "Good guess."

SEVENTY—SIX

GRADE TWELVE STUDENT "Sir, when did you get your first car?"

ME "When I turned seventeen, I bought a seventy-six Ford Capri."

HIM "New or used?"

ME "How old do you think I am?"

YOLO

A grade twelve student enters class wearing a shirt with *YOLO* in huge letters on the front of it.

ME "Are you serious?"

HER "What's wrong with it? YOLO, sir."

ME "But you said you were Hindu. You told me you believe in reincarnation."

HER "Yeah. So?"

ME "As you were."

DRIVING LESSON

GRADE TWELVE STUDENT "Sir, can you teach me how to drive?"

ME "I don't think so."

HIM "Why not?"

ME "It'd be weird because I'm, you know ..."

HIM "Asian?"

ME "Your English teacher."

HIM "Oh."

1984

Grade ten students have asked me to describe what my life was like when I was their age.

ME "It was nineteen eighty-four and breakdancing was getting big."

STUDENT "That's like how my grandfather starts stories."

ME "Did he fail you for interrupting his stories?"

ORGANS

A grade ten student has asked me to help him study for his biology test.

ME "The excretory system helps you ..."

HIM "Get it out."

ME "Um, okay. And the reproductive system helps you ..."

HIM "Get it in."

ME "Um, no."

THE CHILDREN

GRADE TEN STUDENT "Sir, why don't you like children?"

ME "I love children."

HER "Then why don't you want any of your own?"

ME "Because they grow into teenagers."

HER "We're teenagers."

ME "Yup."

HER "Oh."

THE CHILDREN, PART 2

THE SAME GRADE TEN STUDENT FROM YESTERDAY "What's so bad about teenagers?"

ME "You know I talk with your parents, right? They tell me about those times you shut your door and don't answer it, how you totally ignore them when they're trying to talk to you, the constant eye-rolling."

HER "I don't do that."

ME "You just did it now."

HER "I did?"

ME "It's like breathing to you, isn't it?"

She storms back to her seat.

ME "See?!"

HEURISTICS

GRADE EIGHT STUDENT "Can you tell more funny stories about yourself for this lesson? It helps us remember."

ME "Okay, then. First, tell me what you remember from our last class about China."

HER "Your girlfriend's Chinese!"

ME "Um, okay. What else?"

HER "You wouldn't tell us anything else about her."

DAYLIGHT SAVINGS

A grade ten student walks into class late.

ME "You're late."

HIM "Daylight savings, sir."

ME "That was two days ago."

HIM "I was really affected."

A DOG'S BREAK

GRADE ELEVEN STUDENT "Sir, you getting away for spring break?"

ME "No. I'm going to try to take my dogs on a different hike every day."

HIM "But it's *your* break, not your dogs'."

ME "I know. But I'm always cognizant of the fact that one day, my dogs will die. And on that day, I know I'll wish I had one more chance to take them on one more hike. I know this. So I don't want any regrets."

HIM "Do you treat your friends like that?"

ME "People aren't as nice as dogs."

HIM "True."

COFFEE BREAK

GRADE TWELVE STUDENT "Sir, how many cups of coffee do you drink a day?"

ME "About five."

HER "That's crazy! That's more than my dad, and he drives a truck. That's got to be bad for you. Why do you drink so much caffeine?"

ME "To keep me awake during your interrogations."

HER "Hey!"

SPRING BREAK

GRADE TWELVE STUDENT "Sir, what are you going to do for spring break?"

ME "I'm not sure. Probably take my dogs out a lot."

HIM "You're not going to party it up?"

ME "Your forties are going to be a great disappointment to you."

ADVICE

GRADE TEN STUDENT "Sir, have you ever thought of using moisturizer on your face?"

ME "No."

HER "You should."

ME "Thanks. Have you ever thought of being a peer counsellor?"

HER "No."

ME "You shouldn't."

PREQUEL

GRADE TEN STUDENT "Sir, what are you writing?"

ME "It's a journal."

HER "What are you writing about?"

ME "Someone said something really funny today."

HER "You write down the stuff we say?"

ME "Whenever I get a chance, yeah."

HER "What for?"

ME "So that when I get older I can look back fondly on these days, and remember you guys and smile."

HER "Am I in there?"

ME "Actually, a few weeks ago ..."

I open to the entry involving her. She reads.

HER "Oh my God! I said that?"

ME "Do you remember this?"

HER "Yeah, but it sounds silly now."

IMPRESSION

GRADE ELEVEN STUDENT "Sir, it's so plain in your room. Maybe you should get some art on the walls or something."

ME "You paint me something and I'll put it up on the wall."

HER "Really?"

ME "Yeah. Make me something impressionistic. Maybe something with a lot of bold colours."

HER "I don't paint to order. It's so tacky."

ME "Why are we talking?"

EGG MCMUFFIN

GRADE EIGHT STUDENT "Sir, what did you have for breakfast?"

ME "Cereal. Why?"

HIM "There's a rumour that you eat an Egg McMuffin every morning on the way to work."

ME "Do you think I'd be in this kind of shape if that were true?"

He's quiet.

ME "Do you think I'd be dumb enough to do that?"

HIM "No."

ME "Good."

I'M KOREAN

GRADE ELEVEN STUDENT "Sir, what does this mean?"

He holds out a piece of paper with some Chinese lettering on it.

ME "Why?"

HIM "I want a tattoo. I just want to make sure it means something cool."

ME "And you're asking *me* for a translation?"

HIM "Yeah."

ME "It means forgetful."

HIM "Damn. That won't work."

PANTS

GRADE NINE STUDENT "Sir, what size pants do you wear?"

ME "Why?"

HER "My dad wants to buy you a gift."

ME "And so your father wants to buy me pants?"

HER "Not really. But he asked me what you liked and I told him pants."

ME "Why'd you tell him that?"

HER "He found it weird, too."

BOYS WILL BE BOYS

I have just handed out textbooks to my English 10 class.

STUDENT "Sir, someone drew in my book."

I walk over to look. Her book is open to a page with a large phallus crudely drawn across it.

ME "Sorry. Go exchange it for another copy."

HER "Why are boys always drawing this kind of stuff in the textbooks?"

ME "I don't know. Boys can be immature."

HER "It's disgusting. Like, who wants *that* to be the first thing they see when they open a book?"

ME "True. So just grab another copy."

HER "It's like that's all they think about."

ME "Good point. Now if you could just—"

HER "Like, you don't see girls drawing their parts in—"

ME "All right! I get it!"

IN MY BEST DE NIRO

GRADE TWELVE STUDENT "Sir, have you seen that movie *Taxi Driver*?"

ME "You talkin' to me?"

He looks behind him to see if there's anyone else I could be talking to.

HIM "Um, yes."
ME "Yeah, I've seen it."

PERSONAL ADVICE

My grade eleven students are filling out questionnaires for their career counselling sessions. One student looks burdened.

ME "Are you having problems with the questions?"
HIM "I don't know what I want to do in the future."
ME "No one does."
HIM "Half the guys here know what they want."
ME "Believe me, they most likely don't. They probably know what they *think* they want, but what they don't know is that most of them will change."
HIM "Really?"
ME "If people knew what they wanted, there'd be no such thing as divorce."
HIM "Is this about me or you now?"
ME "Just trying to help."

THE LONG HAUL

A grade twelve student is talking with me after school about relationships. He's been with his girlfriend for two years.

HIM "Do you think we're going to last?"
ME "I don't know. But I do know that very few high school sweethearts end up together for the rest of their lives."

HIM "But can't you say that about any relationship?"

ME "You might last."

(They are now happily married with children.)

HOROSCOPES

A grade ten student has a newspaper in front of her.

HER "Sir, do you want to hear your horoscope?"

ME "Let me guess. It suggests I keep an open mind about something, or watch out for something, or explore new options."

HER "What's your sign?"

ME "Aquarius."

She reads.

HER "How did you know?"

ME "I'm psychic."

HER "No way!"

LIT CRIT

GRADE TWELVE STUDENT "Sir, what are your favourite novels?"

ME "I have three: *The Remains of the Day*, *Of Human Bondage* and *The Master and Margarita*."

HER "That was quick."

ME "I've been asked that question many times and I've had time to think about it."

HER "How about the books you teach us? Are some of them your favourites?"

ME "*The Grapes of Wrath.*"

HER "That's it?"

ME "We can't afford new books."

HER "So let me get this straight: you always say you want to instill in us a love of literature, but you can't even teach us the literature you love?"

ME "Well, it sounds awful the way you put it."

ALONE

GRADE TWELVE STUDENT "Sir, what do you look for in a first date? Like what makes you want a second one?"

ME "That's complicated. I'm not sure. I think it might be different for everyone. It's way easier to know if there's not going to be a second date."

HIM "Really? Like what?"

ME "If we're at a restaurant and my date treats our server poorly, or doesn't make any eye contact with him when ordering, she might be a person who doesn't treat people well."

HIM "Really? That sounds really picky."

ME "When you're talking about possibly sharing your life with someone, you should be picky."

HIM "That sounds more like a way to end up alone."

ME "I'd rather be alone than spend the rest of my life with someone who makes me wish I were alone."

HIM "That's from your comedy act, right?"

ME "Yeah. Sorry."

GRADE TEN STUDENT "Sir, why are they called *smart*phones? They're not even smart. They're dumb."

ME "Hey, I have an old vest that would go nicely with that joke."

HIM "What joke?"

ME "Never mind."

ADULTHOOD

GRADE NINE STUDENT "Sir, have you ever changed a diaper?"

ME "No."

HER "I have. That means I'm more adult than you."

ME "I guess so. You should tell your mother that when she comes to pick you up after school."

HER "I will!"

STARBUCKS

GRADE TEN STUDENT "Sir, may we go to Starbucks?"

ME "Why would I let you go to Starbucks in the middle of class?"

HER "Because you're a really cool teacher who likes his students to be happy."

ME "But I'm primarily an educator who needs you to focus on the task at hand."

HER "But isn't Starbucks from *Moby-Dick* or something? Isn't that literary?"

ME "Right now, it's more fantasy."

HER "And I thought you were cool."

BUMP

GRADE TEN STUDENT "Yo, sir, give it up."

He holds out his fist. I just stare at it.

ME "I'll fist-bump you when you get at least a C-plus."
HIM "What do I get until then?"
ME "Didn't you see me nod at you?"
HIM "Aw, man."

YEARBOOK WRITE-UPS

The grade twelves are working on their grad write-ups for the yearbook. I'm reading one student's very brief sentence.

ME "Is this it?"
HIM "Yup."
ME "A bit inappropriate for your last words in school, don't you think?"
HIM "That's how I want to be remembered."
ME (Reading) "'For the ladies.'"

He shrugs.

ME "What exactly is for the ladies?"
HIM "Me."
ME "Really?"
HIM "It's either that or this."

He points to a sentence farther down the sheet.

I read.

ME "Yeah, go with your first one."

THE HORROR

A grade twelve student storms into class during the break.

HER "Sir, you told my dad that you had to take away my iPhone cuz I used it during class?"

ME "Yup."

HER "Why? Why would you do that?"

ME "What's the big deal?"

HER "He said he's going to downgrade my data plan!"

ME "Wow. What are you going to do with your life now? That's awful."

HER "I know!"

ME "I mean, how will you live?"

HER "I know!"

ME "Your dad sounds like a tyrant."

HER "Why are you laughing?"

ME "Because I'm going to write about this one day."

THE N-WORD

A student raises her hand in the middle of note-taking.

GRADE EIGHT STUDENT "Sir, what's that N-word you said earlier?"

ME "Excuse me?"

She looks confused at my reaction.

ME (Calmer) "Um, what are you trying to describe?"

HER "The person who tells the story."

ME "Narrator."

HER "Thanks."

CHALK IT UP

GRADE NINE STUDENT "Sir, why do you still use chalk?"

ME "Because the school hasn't installed whiteboards yet."

HIM "Chalk's bad for your health."

ME "Well, I'm still standing, aren't I?"

HIM "Yeah, but for how much longer? It's not like you're that young anymore."

ME (Holding out the chalk to him) "Why don't you take a turn at the board?"

MIXED WEATHER REPORT

During a heavy snowfall, a grade ten student pokes his head into my classroom from the hallway.

HIM "Sir, is that snow or water outside?"

ME "Both."

HIM (Reporting back to his buddies) "Hey guys, it's both!"

RESEARCH SKILLS

GRADE NINE STUDENT RETURNING FROM THE LIBRARY "Sir, I can't do any research."

ME "Why not?"

HER "The internet's down."

ME "So you can't do any research?"

HER "Yeah."

ME "In the *library*?"

HER (Louder) "Yeah!"

VOCABULARY LESSON

During a discussion with a grade twelve class on the role of the Senate.

ME "Putting aside their initial purpose, what role do you think they serve now?"

STUDENT "I find their role egregious."

ME "In what way?"

HIM "In every way."

ME "Can you be more specific? How is their role egregious?"

HIM "Um ..."

ME "Did you just learn that word?"

HIM "Yeah."

ME "Good effort."

LIES AND MORE LIES

GRADE TWELVE STUDENT "Sir, how old are you again?"

ME "Forty-four."

HER "Wow. You look like you're about thirty-five."

ME (Jokingly) "And that's an A for you."

ANOTHER STUDENT "I think you look twenty-five."

ME "And you just dropped a grade for that obvious lie."

HIM "But you always tell us to dream big."

ME "And that brings you back to passing."

HIM "Awesome!"

ROBIN WILLIAMS

In March 2006, I had the pleasure of sharing a small comedy stage with Robin Williams. It was the highlight of what had been a nascent comedy career at the time. (I used to be a stand-up comedian and for a few years was one half of a critically acclaimed sketch duo with comedian and author Charlie Demers—who is also my editor on this very book.)

After our sets, I stepped outside for some fresh air and decided not to bother Mr Williams, since he was understandably surrounded by a large number of appreciative fans and comedians.

Twenty minutes later, my sketch partner's girlfriend found me and said, "Robin wants to meet you." I thought she was kidding but then remembered that she's awful at telling lies.

I went inside and found him at the back of the club. Robin Williams is still the warmest, most gracious celebrity I have ever met. He had some very generous things to say about our act and my part in it. We talked about some other things, including our choices in shoes and cycling. He also asked what I did when I wasn't performing, and I told him I was an English teacher.

And then, when no one else was within earshot, I made an attempt to speak from the heart. I wanted this man to know the impact he'd made on me through his art.

ME   "I'm sure you've heard this a million times, but *Dead Poets Society* was one of the things that helped me decide to be an English teacher."

HIM   "Hey, that's not my fault."

And we laughed.

APRIL

GOOD FRIDAY

GRADE NINE STUDENT "Sir, I don't get why we have Friday off."

ME "It's Good Friday."

HIM "What is that?"

ME "It's the day Jesus died."

HIM "Shouldn't they call it Bad Friday or something like that, then?"

ME "It's good because he comes back to life three days later."

HIM "Then what's the big deal?"

ME "You know you can ask your dad these questions."

EASTER

GRADE NINE STUDENT "Sir, I don't understand Easter."

ME "It's a Christian celebration of Jesus's resurrection for humanity's salvation."

He stares at me blankly.

ME "You see, there's this thing Christians call sin that has to be wiped off the slate, as it were."

He's not getting it.

ME "Exactly what part of Easter don't you understand?"

HIM "Why do they hide painted eggs?"

ME "I've got no idea."

FRAGILITY

The last bell rings, and after the students clear the room, a former student walks into the class. He is pushing a stroller.

ME "Oh my God."

HIM "Yeah, I know. Sir, this is Ella."

I'm in shock. He only graduated two years ago.

ME "How old is she?"
HIM "Six months."

He picks her up and shows her to me. She is beautiful.

HIM "You want to hold her?"
ME "I'm not good with babies."
HIM "I wasn't either."

He hands her to me. She coos as I cradle her. Everything about her feels so fragile, and I am overwhelmed with sadness and joy for her father.

ME "What are you doing these days?"
HIM "I'm working three jobs. Saving up for school. I'm going to do that construction program you talked about."
ME "That's amazing. Good for you. I'm so proud of you."

We stay silent a while.

ME "How do you do it?"
HIM "Remember when you told us that one day, if we're lucky, we'll find out we're way stronger than we thought we were?"
ME "I don't remember."
HIM "Well, you did."
ME "And was I right?"
HIM "I don't know yet. I hope so."

SUCK-UP

GRADE NINE STUDENT "Sir, that sweater looks great on you."

ME "You're barely getting a C. All this sucking up's not going to improve your grade."

HIM "I could get a higher C. Like, a super C."

The class starts laughing. He's confused.

ME "You know you could have gone with C-plus."

HIM "Oh yeah."

RESURRECTED

GRADE TEN STUDENT "Sir, was Jesus a zombie?"

ME "No."

HER "But he came back to life?"

ME "According to the Christian tradition, yes."

HER "So, he died, then came back. Doesn't that make him a zombie?"

ME "No. But he did feed a few thousand people with a few loaves of bread and two brains."

I hold up a hand for a high-five. She's standing with her arms folded.

ME "No, he wasn't a zombie."

VCR

GRADE EIGHT STUDENT "Sir, what's the scariest movie you've ever seen?"

ME "Well, I was just a kid, but I remember when my friend bought *Alien*. The day he popped it into the VCR is probably—"

HIM "The what?"

ME "VCR. It played videocassettes."

He's quietly counting in his head.

ME "I'm forty-four."
HIM "Wow. But—"

I can see him thinking.

ME "It was in colour."
HIM "Cool."

PLAYA

GRADE TWELVE STUDENT "Sir, how many times have you fallen in love?"
ME "Too many to count."
HIM (To his buddy) "See? He was a playa."
ME "No. I was a fool."
GRADE TWELVE GIRL "Same thing."

I high-five her.

THE MAN

GRADE TEN STUDENT "Sir, what's the difference between a myth and a legend?"
ME "I'm not sure. I've been called both."

She stares at me blankly.

ME "The definitions are on page nineteen."

ONLINE GAMBLING

GRADE TEN STUDENT "Sir, do you online game?"

ME "No. I don't like the idea of being called awful things by some thirteen-year-old in Arkansas."

HIM "Totally! I've been called—"

ME "Stop. I think 'awful things' covered everything you're about to say."

HIM "I don't know. Some of the stuff I hear is—"

ME "We get it."

GUEST SPEAKER

GRADE ELEVEN STUDENT AFTER LEAVING AN ASSEMBLY "Man, that guy swore a lot."

ME "The guest speaker?"

HIM "Yeah."

ME "What do you think about that?"

HIM "It kind of bugged me the way he thought it was the first time any of us had heard an adult swear, like it was a big deal or something."

ME "Did it distract from his message?"

HIM "What message?"

ME "I'll send him a note."

UNCLE

GRADE NINE STUDENT "Can we call you Uncle instead of Sir?"

ME "Why?"

HER "Cuz of your grey hair. It's like my uncle's."

ME "No, but you can shut up."

GENTLEMEN

GRADE EIGHT STUDENT "Sir, what's a gentleman?"

ME "Remember when the new girl arrived and she didn't have a pen and you loaned her one?"

HIM "Yeah."

ME "That was a gentleman right there."

HIM "Then what's a dude?"

ME "A dude would have done the same thing but then tried to ask her to the spring dance after."

HIM (A light goes on) "Oh. Then I'm happy being a gentleman."

ME "Me, too."

SAVE THE DETAILS

ME "Why are you late?"

GRADE EIGHT STUDENT "Sorry, sir, I was taking a serious dump."

ME "Excuse me?"

HIM (Nervous) "Oh, sorry, I mean poo."

ME "No."

HIM "Uh, a number two?"

DISNEY

GRADE NINE STUDENT "Sir, have you ever been to Disneyland?"

ME "Yup. Why?"

HIM "I've never gone."

ME "Well, I don't think you're missing out. And you're probably too old to enjoy it now."

HIM (Upset) "Great. Another thing I'm never going to do."

ME "This is not the direction I thought this would go."

TAGGING

I catch a grade eight student writing graffiti on his desk.

ME "What do you think you're doing?"

HIM "Yo, sir, that's my tag."

ME "Your mom still drives you to soccer practice and packs your lunches. The only tag for you involves lasers and a toy gun."

HIM "Aw, man."

ME "Now erase that before I call your father."

HIM "Yes, sir."

HALL PASS

GRADE NINE STUDENT "Sir, may I use the hall pass?"

ME "Where are you going?"

HIM "Just want to go for a walk."

ME "I can't give you the hall pass just to stroll through the halls."

She looks like she's been having a rough morning.

ME "But if you need to go to the restroom, you can have the hall pass."

HER "I don't need to go to the restroom."

ME "I don't think you get me. I'm saying (clearing my throat) you can have the hall pass to go walk to the restroom."

HER "But I really just want to go for a walk."

ME "Take the hall pass."

EINSTEIN OR HULK

GRADE NINE STUDENT "Sir, what would you rather be: as smart as Einstein or as strong as the Hulk?"

ME "If I choose the Hulk, do I have his intelligence or keep my own?"

HIM "You keep your own."

ME "Do I have the Hulk's strength without going into a full-on rage?"

HIM "Yup."

ME "Do I keep my size, or when I use my strength, do I grow larger?"

HIM "You stay the same. Just his strength."

ME "Good. Because I can't keep buying new pants every time I want to show off my strength."

HIM "I wasn't expecting this to take so long."

ME "Then you shouldn't have asked such a serious question."

SUCH CONCERN

GRADE ELEVEN STUDENT "Sir, how're you doing?"

ME "I'm fine, thanks."

HIM "You look a bit sick. You feeling okay?"

ME "We're going to have the test today."

HIM "Hey, I'm offended that you think that's the only reason I was asking. How do you know I'm not really concerned about your health?"

I'm staring at him.

HIM "Okay, I really don't care."

CANDID CAMERA

A grade eight student holds a page of Chinese writing in front of me.

HER "Can you read this?"

ME "It's in Chinese."

HER "Yeah."

ME "I'm Korean."

HER "But you told us you don't read Korean."

ME "Is there a hidden camera in here? It feels like there should be."

FALLING IN LOVE

GRADE ELEVEN STUDENT "Sir, you've fallen in love, right?"

ME "Oh, many times."

HIM "How did you know you were in love?"

ME "Because I was certain of it at those times and no one could have talked me out of it."

HIM "Why in the world would you want to be talked out of it?"

ME "You'll see when you fall in love."

TO BOLDLY GO ...

Two grade nine students are in the middle of an argument.

ME "What are you two going on about?"

STUDENT 1 "He thinks time travel is possible, and I say it's not."

STUDENT 2 "There's lots of things people thought weren't possible that ended up being real."

STUDENT 1 "But you'd have to approach the speed of light, and there's no way that's going to happen for us."

ME "You both make good points, but maybe we can keep our voices down?"

STUDENT 1 "But this is important!"

ME (Looking heavenward) "Beam me up, Scotty!"

STUDENT 2 "Who are you talking to?"

A SEXUAL REPRODUCTION

A grade nine student is doing his science work in my class during lunch.

HIM "Sir, do you know how many orgasms there are in asexual reproduction?"

ME "Do you mean organisms?"

He looks down at his text.

HIM "Yeah."

CARPE DIEM

GRADE TWELVE STUDENT "Sir, when are you going to retire?"

ME "I'm not sure. I didn't start saving for my retirement until quite late."

HIM "Why's that?"

ME "For most of my life so far, I've lived as if each day were my last."

HIM "And then what happened?"

ME "I suddenly realized I might live past tomorrow."

SMOKING

GRADE ELEVEN STUDENT "Sir, you ever smoke?"

ME "Yes. Started when I was your age."

HIM "What made you start?"

ME "I saw a movie called *Now, Voyager* starring Bette Davis. There was this French actor named Paul Henreid. Super suave. He put two cigarettes in his mouth and lit both of them and handed one to Davis. I thought, *Man, I want to do that one day*."

HIM "Did you?"

ME "Tried it at a party with this girl I liked. When I handed the cigarette to her, she only said, 'Ewww!'"

HIM "Man, you broke your heart and your lungs in one go."

NOT THE LESSON I PLANNED

I have just read an old news item to my English 8 class about a resourceful six-year-old orphan in China who lives by himself and does all his own cooking and foraging. He lives alone because he has AIDS and no one from the nearby village will go near him, though a few kind-hearted villagers help him occasionally.

ME "What has this story shown you?"

STUDENT "I'll never be as smart as a Chinese kid."

ALMOST ...

I have found one of my grade nine students selling pencils outside his locker to grade twelves on their way to class.

ME "You know you're not allowed to sell things here."

HIM "Hey, it's better than dealing drugs."

ME   "Now, why are those your only two choices?"

HIM   "Society."

ME   "Society, eh? What do you mean by that?"

HIM   "Um ... you know. *Society*."

ME   "You just going to repeat that and hope it eventually makes sense?"

HIM   "Maybe."

AS YOU SAY

GRADE NINE STUDENT   "Sir, how often do you go to the dentist?"

ME   "It's been years since my last visit."

HER   "Wow. That's awful. Didn't you tell us before that we should see our dentist at least once a year?"

ME   "On this topic, do as I say, not as I do."

HER   "How about we do as you do, not as you say."

ME   "How do you know what I do?"

HER   "You just said it."

CLASSICS

GRADE TWELVE STUDENT   "Sir, this book seriously sucks."

ME   "Jane Austen is beloved around the world, and her novels are considered classics. Just give it a chance."

HIM   "If I was interested in a bunch of boring people who do nothing and gossip all day, I could hang around the cafeteria."

MEMBERS ONLY: EIGHTIES STYLE

GRADE TWELVE STUDENT "Sir, where did you get that jacket?"

His buddies are laughing at me.

ME "This is my friend's Members Only jacket. We all used to wear these in the eighties."

HIM "What was the membership to?"

ME "An exclusive club of cool dudes."

HIM "Now we know you're lying."

LOVE POEM

A grade nine student is working on something at his desk during lunch.

HIM "Sir, what rhymes with love?"

ME "Writing a poem?"

HIM "Yeah."

ME "Is it for that girl you were telling me about? Didn't you just start dating?"

HIM "Yeah."

ME "And you want to tell her you love her already?"

HIM "I didn't think about that."

ME "Nothing wrong with taking your time on this."

He looks down at his paper.

HIM "Then what rhymes with make out?"

OMNISCIENCE

A grade eleven student has been sitting idle at her desk during the lesson while her peers have been copying the notes on the board.

ME "So, you're just going to memorize all that without taking notes?"

HER "I've already got it."

She pulls out her cellphone and shows me a photo of the board.

ME "Have you been doing this all year?"

HER "Yup."

ME "How did I not notice that?"

HER "You think you see everything, but you don't. You're not God, sir."

ME "Thanks for the reminder."

G-STRING

A grade eleven student walks up to me with his buddy, both already giggling.

HIM "Sir, I hear you play guitar."

ME "Yup."

HIM "You ever break your G-string?"

They are trying their best to hold back the chuckles.

ME "Yes, yes."

HIM "Did it hurt when you broke your G-string?"

ME "Of course. Go on."

HIM "When you broke your G-string and it snapped, did it—?"

He can't think of what to say.

HIS BUDDY "Did it hurt your bum?"

THE FIRST STUDENT (To his buddy) "That's stupid. Why'd you say that?"

ME "You guys really had to plan that?"

A DISCUSSION

GRADE TEN STUDENT "Sir, I don't get this question."

ME "That question's asking you to discuss one of the main themes of the short story."

HIM "How do I discuss it when it's only me writing it? Doesn't it take two to discuss something?"

ME "A discussion also means a detailed written or oral analysis of something."

HIM "Damn."

ME "Didn't read the story, did you?"

HIM "I tried."

A QUESTION IN THE WIND

While marking some essays at my desk during lunch, a large, muscular student pokes his head into my classroom.

HIM "Sir, what does it mean when someone asks if you were born in a barn?"

ME "It's a way of calling someone ignorant."

HIM "He's dead!"

And like that—he's gone.

HIP HOP

GRADE NINE STUDENT "Sir, did you listen to hip hop when you
 were our age?"

ME "Only when I was dancing."

HIM "So all the time?"

ME "It's like you were there."

LANGUAGES

GRADE TWELVE STUDENT "Sir, do you speak Chinese or Japanese?"

ME "Neither."

HIM "Oh, you were born here?"

ME "No. In Korea."

HIM "Oh."

HIS BUDDY "Awkward!"

SOCKS

GRADE NINE STUDENT "Sir, why aren't you wearing socks?"

ME "I don't wear socks with loafers."

HER "Why not?"

ME "I don't know. Ask the eighties."

HER "How?"

ME "Never mind."

DON'T ASK

GRADE ELEVEN STUDENT "Sir, back in your day, who paid for
 a first date?"

ME "Usually the guy did."

HIM "But what if you're not really into her?"

ME "Um, then don't ask her out on a date in the first place."

HIM "Ah, old-school."

IT'S A SAYING?

A grade twelve student hands in his assignment a day late.

ME "It's late."

HIM "You know what they say: homework today better than homework tomorrow."

ME "Who says that?"

HIM "Me. Just now."

KISS

GRADE ELEVEN STUDENT "Sir, what's the first album you ever bought?"

ME "Kiss, *Destroyer*."

HIM "Is that the name of the band?"

ME "What?"

HIM "Kiss Destroyer. That's a cool name."

ME "No, no. Kiss is the name of the band."

HIM "That's a stupid name."

ME "You're kidding."

HIM "You're telling me if you had a band, you'd rather call it Kiss instead of Kiss Destroyer?"

ME "You've got a point."

JUST ANSWER

Two grade ten students approach me.

STUDENT "Sir, if you could buy any car, what would you buy?"

ME "Hmm, that's a tough one. I'd probably feel guilty if it was too expensive. It would have to be practical. Something good off-road that could fit both my dogs. Maybe a Land Rover?"

HIM "Thanks."

While they're walking away ...

HIS BUDDY "See? I told you he can't give a simple answer to anything."

GANGSTAS

GRADE NINE STUDENT "Sir, did you have gangstas back in your day?"

ME "No. We had gangsters."

HIM "What's the difference?"

ME "I'm not sure. I think it depends on how high you wear your pants."

GUITAR GUY

GRADE TWELVE STUDENT "Sir, was it your sense of humour that won over your girlfriend?"

ME "Partly. But if you ask her, she'd say it was the night we were at a party and I was singing with a guitar."

HER "Gross. You're one of *those*!"

ME "Why do I open myself up to you guys?"

EYELASHES

I see two grade eight girls exchanging money in class.

ME "What's going on here?"

STUDENT 1 "She's selling me fake eyelashes."

ME "You're in grade eight. Why in the world do you need fake eyelashes? Your lashes are fine."

STUDENT 1 "But these are better."

ME "What are you going to do? Bat your eyelashes at some grade eight boy, and then what? He's going to give you a ride home on his handlebars?"

STUDENT 2 "Ew. Who dates grade eight boys?"

I turn to the boy sitting in front of them.

ME "Are you going to just sit there and take this?"

HIM "I don't have a bike."

JOKING

GRADE TWELVE STUDENT "Sir, how did hockey become our national pastime?"

ME "Not sure, but I've got a feeling the Canadian Dental Association had a lot to do with it."

HIM "You're kidding."

ME "Of course. How did you not know that was a joke?"

HIM "Cuz jokes usually make me laugh."

ME "Good one."

ROLLING THE DICE

GRADE TWELVE STUDENT "Sir, if you don't have kids, aren't you
   worried about who's going to take care of you when
   you're old?"

ME "Having kids is no guarantee of that."

HER "Don't you want the possibility, at least?"

ME (Quietly) "Look around this class. Imagine that if you had
   a child, it could be any one of them. *Any one* of them will be
   caring for you when you're old. Would you roll the dice?"

She looks around.

HER "I see what you're saying."

TOO TEXTUAL

GRADE TWELVE STUDENT "Sir, what would you do if you asked a girl
   out and she didn't text back?"

ME "You asked her out by text?"

HIM "Yeah."

He shows me his text.

ME "Well, at least you didn't use any emojis."

He scrolls down farther.

ME "Wow."

LAWYERS

GRADE TWELVE STUDENT "Sir, what did you think you were going to do when you were our age?"

ME "I thought I wanted to be a lawyer."

HIM "What made you change your mind?"

ME "I met some lawyers."

Most of the students laugh. He looks confused.

HIM "So, they gave you good advice or something?"

YOURS?

A grade ten student sees me get out of my car in the staff parking lot.

HIM "Sir, is that your car?"

I look at my car and slowly look back at him.

ME "Are those your shoes?"

He looks down at his feet and back at me.

HIM "Pretty good, sir."

IT ALL BEGAN WITH DURAN DURAN

During a discussion about the advent of music videos and their effect on pop culture I show a clip of an early Duran Duran video.

GRADE TEN STUDENT "Sir, who's that?"

ME "That was one of the greatest musical groups from the eighties: Duran Duran. They helped cement MTV's position in pop culture."

HIM "You liked them?"

ME "Yeah, I did. I even tried to dress like them."

HIM "And was it hard not punching yourself?"

ME "No. It was as hard as failing yourself in English."

HIM "Oh."

YO MAMA

GRADE NINE STUDENT "Sir, do you know any yo mama jokes?"

ME "Yo mama is so nice that she packed that amazing lunch for you today."

HIM "That's not funny."

ME "No, it isn't, because you have no idea what mothers go through to make sure your belly's full. It's no laughing matter."

After some quiet consideration ...

HIM "Sir, yo mama's so—"

ME "Don't."

HIM "Okay."

THE RULE

GRADE NINE STUDENT (Giggling) "Sir, why aren't Asians good at hockey?"

ME "That's an old joke and it's racist."

HIM "No, not if you're Asian."

ME "But you're not Asian."

HIM "I know, but you are."

ME "I don't think you get how it works."

KATHARINE HEPBURN

GRADE TWELVE STUDENT "Sir, who's your favourite actress?"

ME "Katharine Hepburn."

HER "What's she in?"

ME "She's in a lot. *The Philadelphia Story* is one of my favourites."

HER "Is that the one about AIDS?"

ME "No. You're thinking of *Philadelphia*. That was Tom Hanks."

HER "You sure?"

ME "Are you asking if I'm sure that I'm not mixing up my favourite actress with Tom Hanks?"

HER "You make my question sound stupid."

ALLERGIES

I've just finished sneezing a few times in my English 9 class.

STUDENT "You have a cold, sir?"

ME "Allergies."

HIM "What are you allergic to?"

ME "Probably pollen."

HIM "Where's the pollen? We're indoors."

ME "It's in the air."

HIM "Then how do you know it's pollen? It could be anything. You could be allergic to oxygen."

ME "It only happens this time of year when the pollen's heavy."

HIM "Or it could be something in the air that happens to come around when the pollen does."

ME "It's possible."

HIM "Wow. You give up so easy."

OUT OF AFRICA

GRADE TWELVE STUDENT "Sir, what's your favourite movie of all time?"

ME *"Out of Africa."*

HIM "Why that one?"

ME "Meryl Streep plays this strong, intelligent, independent woman, and I kind of fell in love with her character. It made me want to be with someone like that."

HIM "Was she hot?"

ME "You probably won't like the movie."

STANDING TALL

GRADE EIGHT STUDENT "Sir, the teacher in home ec today yelled at the class."

ME "Were the students behaving badly?"

HIM "Yeah. They weren't listening to her."

ME "But you listened, right?"

HIM "Yes, sir."

ME "Because you're a young man, not a boy, right?"

HIM "No. Because I have no friends in that class."

ME "Oh."

ALIENS

GRADE ELEVEN STUDENT "Sir, do you believe there's life on other planets?"

ME "Sure, why not?"

HIM "Really?"

ME "I don't really care either way."

HIM "How does it not blow your mind?"

ME "There's life on this planet none of us really cares about. So why care about life up there that we'll have no chance of seeing?"

HIM "I care about all life."

ME "What are the names of all your neighbours?"

HIM "Good point."

ANIMAL, VEGETABLE OR ...

In the middle of a brainstorming exercise, I suddenly point at a grade eight student.

ME "Quick! Name your favourite animal."

HIM "Pokémon!"

The students erupt in laughter.

ME "I'm surprised you didn't choose a shark or something."

HIM "Me too."

VAMPIRES

The English 9 class is discussing vampires in literature.

ME "So the most common way to kill a vampire is with a stake through the heart."

STUDENT "Sir, how would that work?"

ME "With a hammer, I suppose, or a very strong downward thrust."

HIM "You'd have to be pretty strong."

ME "I think someone with average strength could do it."

HIM (Laughing) "Sure! I'd like to see you try."

The other students look confused.

ME "You realize we're talking about a sharp stick, right?
S-T-A-K-E. Not S-T-E-A-K."

HIM "Oh. You should have just said 'sharp stick' then."

THE RUN

Overheard in English 8 ...

STUDENT 1 "Hey, what are we doing in gym class today?"

STUDENT 2 "We're doing the big run today. About five kilometres."

Student 1 looks stressed. Student 2 knows that Student 1 gets teased occasionally about his weight.

STUDENT 2 "Hey, I'll run with you. It'll be fun."

STUDENT 1 "Really? Awesome."

And this is why I often just sit back and let them teach me things I've forgotten.

VEGAS, BABY!

STUDENT 1 "My dad is getting remarried in Las Vegas."

STUDENT 2 "Why Las Vegas?"

STUDENT 1 "I'm not sure."

STUDENT 2 "Sir, why would his father go to Las Vegas to get married?"

ME "All I know is what happens in Vegas stays in Vegas."

STUDENT 1 (Panicked) "My father is moving to Vegas?!"

ASSIGNED SEATING

GRADE NINE STUDENT "Sir, can I sit next to Bobby today?"

ME "You know I don't assign seats. Help yourself."

He looks shocked. His classmates start laughing.

HIM "When did this start?"

ME "On the first day when I told all of you to sit wherever you want."

HIM "Was I here?"

ME "You're the one who sat on the floor and everyone laughed."

HIM "I did that?"

I nod.

HIM "Wow, I'm good."

CLOSER

I'm showing a scene from *Macbeth* in English 11.

STUDENT "Sir, I can't see the TV from back here."

ME "Why don't you move closer to the front?"

HIM "I've got a better idea. Why don't you get a bigger TV?"

ME "Not bad. But I've got an even better idea."

HIM "Never mind! I'm moving."

His classmates are laughing as he good-naturedly jogs to a closer desk. I give him a pat on the back.

HIM "I know I can act like an idiot, but I'm not stupid."

CLOSER, PART 2

The same English 11 student sees me immediately walk to my desk and write in my teaching journal.

HIM "You writing what I said?"

ME "Yes. It was hilarious."

HIM (Nodding approvingly, in his best Matthew McConaughey) "All right, all right, all right."

YOUNG JEDI

I am handing assignments back to my English 9 class.

STUDENT (Surprised by his mark) "An A!"

ME "It was a masterful job, young Jedi."

HIM "I'm Corey."

ME "What?"

HIM "I'm Corey, not Jedi."

ME "Sorry. May the force be with you."

HIM (To another student, quietly) "What's wrong with him?"

UNDER THE SADNESS

One of my grade nine students is having a bad day. She already has a detention with me for being late.

ME "Not going well today, eh?"

HER "Not really."

ME "Is everything okay at home?"

HER "No. My parents are fighting again and I don't know what to do."

ME "What's going on?"

HER "My dad hasn't seen me in a long time, so wants to take me for the long weekend, but my mom is saying no."

ME "Wow. I wish I had people fighting over me. They both must love you like crazy."

HER "I guess so."

ME "Is that why you were late today?"

HER "What do you mean?"

ME "Were you late because you couldn't sleep last night because of your parents?"

HER "No, I just hit snooze too many times."

ME "Well, you could have totally taken advantage of that. Why don't we cancel your detention for your honesty, but next time you're late, we double it and you have to listen to eighties music during the whole time?"

HER "Thanks, sir."

MUHAMMAD

GRADE NINE STUDENT "Sir, is there anyone alive today who has met Muhammad?"

Her classmates start laughing.

ME "Does that answer your question?"

HER (Laughing at herself) "Oh, yeah. Cuz he's royalty or something, right?"

ME "You really need to start paying attention to these dates."

LORD OF THE FLIES

ME "So why do these kids decide to use the conch during meetings?"

GRADE ELEVEN STUDENT "Wait, sir, are they holding it?"

ME "Yes."

HIM "That's gross."

ME "Well, I'm sure it's not slimy or anything."

HIM "Oh, man! I'd puke. I just wouldn't say anything."

ME "What do you think a conch is?"

HIM "Um ... underwear?"

The class starts laughing.

ME "You're thinking of gonch."

His buddies are howling now.

ME "Why would they hold up someone's underwear in meetings?"

HIM "It would get *my* attention."

ZOOLANDER, JR.

GRADE TEN STUDENT "I wouldn't mind modelling this summer to make some money."

ME "You're a good-looking guy. Maybe talk to your parents about it."

HIM "And I heard you don't have to be gay."

I look at him. He's not joking.

ME "No. You don't have to be gay."

HIM "It's cool they accept everyone."

MOTHER—SON MOMENT

A grade twelve student whom I've never met walks into my classroom in the middle of a lesson.

HIM "Do I look high?"

ME "No."

HIM "Good, cuz my mom's about to pick me up and she'll kill me if I'm high."

He leaves. The class of bewildered grade twelves starts laughing.

GRADE TWELVE STUDENT "Sir, he totally looked high."

ME "I know."

FISHING FOR MEANING

A grade twelve student is showing his classmates his new tattoo on his arm.

ME "What does that mean?"

HIM "It's a fish."

ME "I can see that. Does it hold any significance for you?"

HIM "I like fish."

ME "I know. But is it symbolic of anything?"

HIM "Um ... all fish?"

ME "Thank you. Money well spent."

HISTORICAL CONTEXT

During a documentary on China's first emperor, when the actor shows up onscreen.

GRADE EIGHT STUDENT "Sir, when was video invented?"
ME "No, that's not really him."
HIM "Okay, thanks."

SIBLINGS

GRADE TWELVE STUDENT "Man, I can't wait for my bro to go back in."
ME "Back in where?"
HER "Jail."
ME "Why would you want that?"
HER "Cuz he never lets me party when he's out. He's like a dad."
ME "Yes. Exactly like one."

SHAVE

GRADE TWELVE STUDENT "Sir, why are you growing a beard?"
ME "I'm not. Just been too lazy to shave this week."
HER "It makes you look like a hipster, but you're way too old to be a hipster, so you should probably shave."
ME "It's going to be funny when you're way too old to be a grade twelve student."
HER "What?"
ME "Never mind."

YOU JOKER, YOU

During a grade nine lesson about Turkish rule in India.

ME   "Has anyone here been to Delhi?"

Three Indian students and one Latino boy raise their hands.

ME   (To the Latino kid) "You've been to Delhi?"
HIM   "I go there almost every day for lunch."
ME   (Laughing) "Good one."
HIM   "What?"
ME   "Oh, you're serious."

NUANCE

ME   "Where were you last class?"
GRADE TWELVE STUDENT   "You said I didn't have to come."
ME   "No. You asked me if you had to come to class and I said you don't *have* to do anything."
HIM   "Oh."
ME   "Come see me after school."
HIM   "Do I have to?"

I stare at him.

HIM   "Got it."

HISTORY

The last bell of the day has rung and one of my students from English 12 hasn't left his seat.

ME   "Is something wrong?"

HIM   "Sir, I don't know what to do."

ME   "What do you mean?"

HIM   "I'm graduating next month and I don't know what I'm going to do."

I sit in the desk next to him.

ME   "Do you want to work? Do you want to study?"

HIM   "I don't know."

ME   "Why don't you go to college and study history? I bet you'd be good at it."

HIM   "History? You kidding? I'm barely passing history."

ME   "That's because you don't like the way it's taught here. It's different in college."

HIM   "How?"

ME   "You know how you're always questioning everything I teach? Like today when I was talking about Romanticism?"

HIM   "Yeah."

ME   "That's what history is: questioning. You're built for it. You don't take anyone's word for anything. You've got a chip on your shoulder. You like uncovering truth and pointing out frauds. Which makes you not built for our type of schooling. But you'd be awesome at history."

HIM   "But I don't even have the marks to get into college. I slacked off this year."

ME "Trust me: you work your butt off until finals, and you'll get into college and you'll excel at history."

HIM "I'll think about it."

That was the last time we talked about it that year. The next time we discussed it was four years later

After he'd received his bachelor of arts with a major in history.

After he'd gotten accepted into the master's program for history at a major university.

He found me teaching at a different school, just to tell me I was right about him.

And that is the best moment I've ever had as a teacher.

DEAD POETS SOCIETY

After showing an English 11 class *Dead Poets Society*.

ME "Well, what did you think of the movie?"

STUDENT "So, you're expecting us to stand on our desks and clap for you at the end of the year? Is that why you're showing it to us? Cuz it ain't happening."

ME "That hurt."

HIM "The truth sometimes does."

PAPER

ME "What are you doing out of your seat?"

GRADE NINE STUDENT "I need paper."

ME "Here, take my paper."

HER "I don't like your paper. It's cheap. You have to stop buying your supplies at the dollar store."

ME "Whatever happened to 'No, thank you'?"

FOLLOW THE LEADER

Two grade ten students walk in late.

ME "Why are you late?"

STUDENT 1 "I lost track of time."

ME (To the other one) "How about you?"

STUDENT 2 "I was just following him."

ME "If he jumped off a bridge, would you, too?"

STUDENT 2 "Like, a big bridge or a small one?"

CHEWBACCA

GRADE NINE STUDENT "Sir, what's a Chewbacca?"

ME "You're kidding me."

He stares at me blankly.

ME "Chewbacca is the name of a Wookiee."

HIM "In hockey?"

ME "What?"

HIM "Does he play hockey?"

ME "Not *rookie*. *Wookiee*."

HIM "Oh. I don't know what that is."

ME "No kidding."

DEVOLUTION

A grade ten student walks into first period ten minutes late.

ME "Why are you late?"

HIM "I had to wait for my mom to drive me."

ME "Don't you live only four blocks away?"

HIM "Yeah, but it's raining."

I take out my phone and start pushing buttons.

HIM "What are you doing?"

ME "I'm texting my mother to let her know I wasn't as lazy as she claimed I was."

TOO WEIRD

GRADE TWELVE STUDENT "Any big plans for the weekend, sir?"

ME "Some dinner. Maybe go to a movie. You?"

HIM "No, thanks. It'd be kind of weird."

ME "Is this your first conversation?"

TECHNO MUSIC

GRADE ELEVEN STUDENT "Sir, are you into techno?"

ME "How'd you guess?"

HER "Cuz you're Asian."

ME "That's so perceptive of you. Cuz most weekends, my friends
and I pump up the techno on our speakers while driving our
souped-up Civics around town, burning rubber on our way to
dim sum in Chinatown."

HER "Really?"

I stare at her.

HER "Oh. You made that up."

ME "Yes."

HER "So ... do you listen—"

ME "I don't listen to techno."

HER "Cool."

STUPID ENGLISH

GRADE ELEVEN STUDENT "English is stupid."

ME "It can often seem that way. Like, the word 'knight'
itself has only one syllable yet contains three silent
consonants."

HIM "No, I mean this course. It's stupid."

ME "Still upset at your marks, eh?"

DE NIRO

GRADE TEN STUDENT "Sir, what's your favourite movie?"

ME "There are a bunch of them. For American movies, probably *The Godfather*. Parts one and two."

HIM "Who's in it?"

ME "You haven't heard of *The Godfather*?"

He shrugs his shoulders.

ME "Al Pacino? Marlon Brando? Robert De Niro?"

HIM "What have they been in?"

ME "You serious?"

He stares at me blankly.

ME "*Raging Bull*? *Mean Streets*? *Taxi Driver*? *Goodfellas*?"

Nothing.

ME (Doing my best De Niro impression) "You talkin' to me?"

He looks confused.

ME "The father in *Meet the Parents*."

HIM "Oh, *him*!"

ME "Jesus."

GUM

GRADE TWELVE STUDENT "Sir, would you like some gum?"

She holds out a pack.

ME (Joking) "Is my coffee breath that bad?"

HER (Upset, looking around at her classmates) "Who told him?!"

I, ROBOT

After showing some grade ten students some old-school breakdance moves after school ...

STUDENT "Sir, I bet you used to be a pretty good dancer."

ME "What do you mean *used to*?"

HIM "Your robot looks like it's low on batteries."

ME "Hey, dance as if no one is watching."

HIM "Well, there's your problem."

RINGER

A cellphone goes off in the middle of my English 10 lesson. The student is embarrassed but not doing anything about it.

ME "You going to turn that off?"

HIM "I don't know how to turn off the ringer."

ME "Let me try."

He hands me the phone. I answer the call.

ME "Hello? (Pause) Hi, this is Mr Bae, his English teacher. (Pause) Yes, he left his ringer on during class. (Pause, then laugher) Yes, he can be at times. But since I have you on the phone, mind if we chat right now about some concerns I have about his work habits? (Pause) Excellent."

HIM "Damn."

DIET

Some students are spending their lunch break in my classroom while I eat and work at my desk.

GRADE ELEVEN STUDENT "Sir, you buy your lunch a lot."

ME "Yeah, I know I should pack my own, but I often run out of time."

HER "That's no excuse. That's all processed food you're eating. At your age, you really need to watch what you eat."

ME "Thank you for your concern. I'll try to do better."

HER "Think about your looks, too. Look at your belly. I don't think it was that big at the beginning of the year."

ME "Where are your friends?"

HER "Oh, they're on their way right now. And I know they'll tell you the same things."

ME "Oh, it's my lucky day."

TO BOLDLY GO ...

Four students I've never met approach me after the last bell.

STUDENT "Sir, we need a teacher to sponsor our *Star Trek* club. Would you be interested?"

ME "What makes you think I'm into *Star Trek*?"

HIM "Our friends told us. You teach them."

ME   "I don't remember ever saying anything of the sort."

HIM   "They said you told them that George Takei is a relative of yours."

ME   "Then they're mistaken. I must have made a joke about it and they thought I was being serious. I'm not even Japanese."

They look at each other, somewhat befuddled. One of the other students pipes up.

HIM   "Did you ever date him?"

GREEKS AND ARMS

We are watching a slide show of ancient Greek sculpture in Humanities 8.

STUDENT   "Sir, why didn't they like arms?"

ME   "Sorry?"

HIM   "Greeks."

I look at the screen and suddenly realize his confusion.

ME   "The arms broke off over the years."

HIM   "So, they used to—"

ME   "Yes, they used to have arms."

HIM   "Okay, good."

FIELD TRIP

After class, one of my English 8 students stays behind to chat with me privately.

HER "Sir, why can't we go on the field trip? It's not fair."

ME "Only half the class got their forms and deposits in on time. I'm truly sorry."

HER "Then can those of us who handed in forms go?"

ME "I need you to really think about this because you're one of the leaders in the class: why do you think only half the class got their deposits and forms in before the deadline?"

She's thinking.

HER "Because half the parents can't afford it?"

ME "Possible. Now, if that's true, how do you think it would make those students feel if the rest of us who could afford it went without them?"

HER "That'd be awful."

I watch her process this.

HER "Can't the school pay for them?"

ME "We don't have that kind of money."

More processing.

HER "Wait. Why don't we find a cheaper field trip?"

ME "Maybe you can help me come up with an idea. I'm not good at this."

HER (Excitedly) "This way, we can all be the same!"

Fifteen minutes later, she decides it would be a good idea if we had a class picnic and I provided most of the food so that those who couldn't bring food wouldn't feel left out.

It was a great picnic.

AND TAXES

GRADE ELEVEN STUDENT (Pointing at a line in a book) "Sir, what does this saying mean?"

ME "What do you think it means?"

HER "But I can think of way more certainties than death and taxes."

ME "Name one."

HER "Love."

ME "Not everyone finds love, or has it."

HER "Everyone has someone in the world waiting to love them. They just need to find each other."

ME "Can I write that down?"

HER "Why?"

ME "I want you to visit me twenty years from now and I'm going to show you what you just said. It'll be hilarious."

REFORMATION

GRADE ELEVEN STUDENT "Wait, Martin Luther was from Germany?"

ME "Yes."

HER "But wasn't he black?"

ME "You're thinking of Martin Luther King, Jr."

HER "So his father was white?"

JFK

I am trying to help a grade ten student pick a historical figure for his project.

ME "How about JFK?"

HIM "Who's that?"

ME "President John F. Kennedy."

He stares at me blankly.

ME "He's the one who was assassinated."

HIM "I don't follow the news."

GODZILLA

GRADE EIGHT STUDENT "Sir, have you seen *Godzilla*?"

ME "The recent version? Not yet."

HIM "You'd like it. It's got a lot of Japanese people in it."

ME "Um, I'm Korean. Remember?"

HIM "Oh yeah."

Awkward silence.

HIM "Godzilla's not Japanese."

SMOKES

A grade twelve student walks into class with a cigarette tucked behind his ear.

ME "You better put that away."

HIM "It's so I don't lose it. It's my last one."

ME "If you don't put it away, the last one you just smoked will be your last one today."

He looks confused. His friend leans over to him.

FRIEND "He's saying he's going to confiscate that smoke."
HIM "Oh."
FRIEND "Or kill you."
HIM "Oh!"

THE HUNGER GAMES

In a discussion of favourite novels with my English 9 class, *The Hunger Games* comes up.

STUDENT "I tried to read that but gave up."
ME "Why? Did it not live up to your expectations?"
HIM "No. I thought it was about competitive eating."

The students laugh.

ME "That's hilarious."
HIM "I wasn't joking."
ME "Oh. That's awful."

DAWG

During an English 9 class, I stop at a student's desk and point at his paragraph.

ME "You spelled dog wrong."
HIM "D-A-W-G. That's a different type of dog."

ME "What does that mean?"

HIM "It's like my boy. My brother."

ME "Why can't you spell it D-O-G?"

HIM "That's a pervert type of dog."

ME "Aren't all dogs kind of like that?"

HIM "Oh yeah. And I guess my friend is, too."

A COLD ONE

GRADE TWELVE STUDENT "Sir, you strike me as a beer man."

ME "How can you tell?"

HIM "Well, though you're easily refined enough for wine, I doubt you'd have the patience to sit around reading about a beverage. You're a man of the people."

I look at the pile of marking I have next to me on my desk.

ME "You know your essay's in that stack, right?"

HIM "Absolutely."

NON SEQUITURS FROM ANOTHER PLANET

My English 10 class is discussing the idea of cultural shifts.

ME "Good stuff so far. Anyone else?"

STUDENT "The sixties."

ME "Good. How was the sixties different?"

HIM "Well, in the US, there used to be lots of alien abductions, but in the sixties it stopped."

There is silence. Then, the students start giggling.

ME   "Okay."

HIM   "You know what I mean, right?"

ME   "To be honest, no."

HIM   "I guess you had to be there."

HELLO, TREES

In the middle of English 11, I notice one of the students staring intently out the window.

ME   "Hey, you okay?"

HIM   (Snapping out of it) "Oh. Sorry, sir."

ME   "What were you staring at out there? There's nothing but trees."

HIM   "If you stare at them long enough, it looks like they're waving at you. But, like, all at once."

ME   "Is it a friendly wave or a menacing wave?"

He looks back out the window. After a few seconds—

HIM   "Friendly."

I lean closer to him so that only he can hear me.

ME   "If you're stoned during my classes, you're going to miss out on a lot of great stuff, and years from now, you'll regret missing this opportunity. Okay?"

HIM   "Thanks, sir."

(He never showed up stoned to my classroom again.

I think.)

BACK TO THE FUTURE

GRADE TWELVE STUDENT "Sir, if you could go back in time and give yourself advice in grade twelve, before you graduate, what advice would you give?"

ME "Why didn't you just ask me what's my best advice for graduating students?"

HIM "I won't get a standard answer this way, and it'll tell me what you were like in high school."

ME "Well, then, I'd tell myself to think more like you."

WISE GUY

GRADE ELEVEN STUDENT "Sir, my next class is all the way over in D-wing."

ME "Then you better get a move on."

HIM "Can you call the teacher and let him know I'll be late?"

ME "He'll know you're late when you show up late."

HIM "But if you call him and tell him I'm late for a good reason, he won't give me a detention."

ME "You don't have a good reason. The bell went three minutes ago and you're still sitting here."

HIM "But I'm in your presence, soaking up wisdom."

ME "Do you think I'm stupid?"

HIM "See? You saw right through me. You're very wise."

EXPLAINING THE EIGHTIES

As a treat, I show graduating students a photo of me from my high school days.

STUDENT "Why was your hair so high?"

ME   "It was the eighties. We thought it was cool."

STUDENT   "What's with the rolled-up sleeves on your suits?"

ME   "That was my Platinum Blonde phase."

STUDENT   "Did you guys know it looked stupid at the time?"

ME   "Are you trying not to graduate from my class?"

CLOUDS

We're having one of our outdoor education classes in the park across the street.

GRADE TWELVE STUDENT   "Sir, you ever look up at the clouds and try to figure out the shapes?"

ME   "To be honest, not anymore."

HER   "Why not?"

ME   "Because I forget to do it."

HER   "How do you forget to do something like that?"

ME   "When you get older, you're going to forget to do a lot of important things."

SWEAT

GRADE TWELVE STUDENT   "Sir, you sweat a lot."

ME   "Yeah, it's hot in here."

HER   "You should do something about that. It's kind of gross."

ME   "I'll get on it. Thanks."

HER   "Did your girlfriend know about your perspiration problem when you first met, or did she find out too late?"

ME   "This is the worst episode of *Oprah* ever."

GYM

GRADE EIGHT STUDENT "Sir, why do boys and girls have separate gym classes?"

ME "I'm not sure. My guess is it's a remnant of an earlier time when people thought boys and girls had incompatible strengths and interests when it comes to physical activity."

HIM "Is it cuz you guys wore tighter shorts back then?"

ME "Or it could be that."

CURIOSITY

GRADE NINE STUDENT "Sir, did you take the bus to work today?"

ME "No."

HIM "Did you cycle here?"

ME "No."

HIM "Did you get a lift from one of the other teachers?"

ME "Are you trying to find out why my car's not in the parking lot?"

HIM "Yeah."

ME "Then why don't you just ask me?"

HIM "Oh. Okay."

I wait.

ME "Well?"

HIM "I don't really need to know."

IN SICKNESS AND IN HEALTH

GRADE TWELVE STUDENT "Sir, what's the secret to a successful marriage?"

ME "I'll let you know whenever I get there."

HIM "But you've been with one woman for seven years."

ME "That's nothing. Wait a few more years to when we've been through sickness, money problems, career struggles and helping our aging parents, and if we're still together by that point, and happy about it, I'll come find you and tell you the secret."

HIM "That might be too late. Maybe I'll ask someone else."

DETENTION SHARK

GRADE ELEVEN STUDENT "Sir, can I cut ten minutes off my detention and make it up tomorrow?"

ME "Why?"

HIM "I've got to catch my bus."

ME "Okay, but then you owe me twenty tomorrow."

HIM "How's that fair?"

ME "It's the interest on the detention that you owe me."

HIM "That's a hundred-percent interest."

ME "Yup. Take it or leave it."

HIM "I'll leave it."

ME "Fine."

A minute later.

HIM "Can I go?"

ME "No."

It is the last class for a group of graduating grade twelves. They call me to the front of the room and present me with a gift. It is a nice bottle of Connemara Irish whiskey.

ME "Who bought this?"

They all point to one of my students. He is six foot three and has a full beard.

ME "Of course. Didn't they ID you?"
HIM "They haven't IDed me since grade ten."
ME "Too much information."

The students laugh.

ME "This is very thoughtful. How did you know I like whiskey?"
HIM "We guessed. You seem like a whiskey guy."
ME "What made you guys think that?"
HIM "Every Friday, you have that look on your face like you really need a drink."

Everyone laughs.

Me too.

IN THE PRESENT

GRADE TWELVE STUDENT "Sir, you should totally get some air conditioning hooked up in here."
ME "Who's going to pay for it?"
HIM "I was just expressing my thoughts. I didn't think that far ahead."

INDEPENDENCE DAY

GRADE TEN STUDENT "Sir, why's it called Independence Day?"

ME "It commemorates America's declaration of independence from British rule back in 1776."

HIM "I mean the movie."

ME "It commemorates the declaration of the movie industry's independence from art."

HIM "Really? The one with aliens?"

AIR CON

GRADE ELEVEN STUDENT "Sir, it's boiling. Why don't we have air conditioning?"

ME "Because we're a public school. We're not about to spend taxpayers' money on air conditioning."

HER "How are we supposed to learn in heat like this? It's not good for our learning."

ME "Kids in India are in crowded classrooms in much hotter conditions and getting As. I think they're fine."

HER "That's cuz they don't know what air conditioning is!"

TWILIGHT

GRADE TEN STUDENT "Sir, can we read *Twilight* in English?"

ME "I'm sure you can. If it gets boring, try reading it in another language."

HER "I meant in English *class*."

ME "Oh, I'm sorry."

HER "Well?"

ME "Oh, we still talking about that? No."

TWILIGHT, PART 2

GRADE ELEVEN STUDENT "Sir, are you Team Edward or Team Jacob?"

ME "Chicago Bears."

HER "You don't get it."

ME "Oh, I get it. And neither of your teams has a decent ground game."

QUAKE

After a schoolwide earthquake preparedness drill …

GRADE TEN STUDENT "That was stupid."

ME "How?"

HIM "Seriously, this building's so old, in a real earthquake, we'd all be dead. What's hiding under our desks going to do?"

ME "Well, I'm sure there'd be some survivors. We just have to prepare for it regardless."

HIM "If the third floor comes crashing down on you, what am I supposed to do? Lift the whole floor off your crumpled body?"

ME "You better. I'm just about to mark your essay."

DORITOS

I'm sitting in the middle of the classroom, eating a bag of Doritos, while the grade elevens work quietly.

GRADE ELEVEN STUDENT "Sir, what's up with that?"

ME "I suspect a few of you are high right now. First one to drool goes to the office."

HER "You're the Devil, Sir."

DURAN DURAN

Two grade ten students have detention with me. It's been ten minutes and I've been blasting eighties music.

STUDENT "Sir, what the hell is this?"

ME "It's called detention."

HIM "I mean, who is this? It's awful."

ME "It's 'Rio' by Duran Duran."

HIM "Can you play something else? Like hip hop or something?"

ME "Really? Okay, you don't know what you're missing. But if you like hip hop, you'll love these guys."

I play "Hold Me Now" by the Thompson Twins.

HIM "Oh God."

WHEN I GROW UP

GRADE ELEVEN STUDENT "Sir, what did you want to be when you grew up?"

ME "Depends on my age. When I was in high school, I wanted to be a lawyer. When I was seven, I wanted to be Superman. And for a brief time when I was four, I wanted to be a dancer."

HER "You were so in touch with yourself for a four-year-old."

ME "Thanks. What?"

FRIENDING

GRADE ELEVEN STUDENT "Sir, I think it'd be cool if we were Facebook friends."

ME "Funny how one man's cool is another man's creepy."

HIM "I don't find you creepy."

ME "I don't think you got it."

SEMANTICS

GRADE NINE STUDENT "Sir, were you a straight-A student?"

ME "I used to be, until my grade twelve year."

HIM "What happened?"

ME "Girls happened."

HIM "I got you, sir."

He fist-bumps me. He's about to walk away when I stop him.

ME "That means I had a crush on a few girls. That's it."

HIM "Oh. I thought you meant—"

ME "I know."

A WHOLE NEW WORLD

GRADE TEN STUDENT "Sir, Disney should totally make some fat princesses."

ME "Good idea. Maybe if young girls saw princesses of varying body types, it would break down the ideas we have of ideal physical beauty."

HIM "Um, I just think it'd be funny."

KINDLING

GRADE ELEVEN STUDENT "Sir, why don't we get with the times and buy Kindles and stuff? Why are we still using real books?"

ME "It would cost money that our district doesn't have."

HIM "Man, but books are so old-school. We're supposed to be the future."

ME "Why do you care? You have yet to finish a single novel for me this year."

HIM "I don't know. I like the look of the Kindles."

ME "That's a frightening thought."

HIM "What?"

ME "You're the future."

HISTORICAL CONTEXT

GRADE TEN STUDENT "Sir, why are we studying history? This is supposed to be English *literature*."

ME "We need the historical context for the next unit."

HIM "Who cares about the history and what cavemen did and all that."

ME "This is the Enlightenment."

HIM "So?"

ME "We're studying history."

HISTORICAL CONTEXT, PART 2

GRADE ELEVEN STUDENT "I still think studying historical writing is a waste of time."

ME "It provides a glance into what people thought during certain periods. Don't you find it the least bit interesting?"

HIM "Who cares what people thought a long time ago? It's like if in the future, someone finds my diary. Think it's going to interest them at all?"

I look deadpan at the rest of the class. They are giggling in anticipation.

ME "You're just going to lob that slow pitch for me, huh?"
HIM "Oh, crap."

STATUS UPDATE

GRADE ELEVEN STUDENT "Sir, Jerry changed my Facebook status behind my back."
ME "Then don't go on Facebook during class time."
HIM "But he wrote that I have a hairy rear end."
ME "I can't do anything about that."
HIM "But you're the teacher!"
ME "Just shave it or wax it. It's none of my business."
HIM "Oh, man."

SHAKESPEAREAN TRAGEDY

GRADE TEN STUDENT "Sir, if I ever opened a Shakespearean-themed deli, I'd have a breakfast item called a Denver Hamlet."
ME "I really wish you could put that level of thought into your essays."

THE GRAND INQUISITOR

GRADE ELEVEN STUDENT "Sir, what's the first book to ever change your thinking?"

ME "Dostoevsky's *The Brothers Karamazov*. That novel shattered me."

HIM "Why?"

ME "I was eighteen and didn't know until then that it was possible to address the big philosophical issues in story form."

HIM "Then why don't we study that one in class?"

ME "It's quite long. I don't think the majority of your classmates would like it. And it's very challenging."

HIM "So, our school doesn't have money for new books?"

ME "If you want to put it that way, yes."

RECURRENCE

GRADE TEN STUDENT "Sir, if you could do it all over again, would you be a teacher?"

ME "What are the parameters? Will I retain the same knowledge I have now in new contexts, or is it just a replay of what's already passed?"

HER "I haven't thought about it."

ME "And if it's the latter, will I also arrive at this moment again?"

HER "You never play games, do you?"

ME "And you never think about time travel."

SELF-ASSESSMENT

GRADE ELEVEN STUDENT "Sir, you believe in pursuing your dreams, right?"

ME "Within reason, yes."

HER "What does that mean?"

ME "Generally, you have to make an honest assessment of your talents, and then go from there."

HER "That's a bit pessimistic, don't you think?"

ME "You ever watch *American Idol*?"

HER "Oh. Got it."

FICTIONAL WORLDS

GRADE ELEVEN STUDENT "Sir, why do we read fiction? It's all make-believe."

ME "There are lots of reasons, but my favourite is that it allows us to imagine the limits of our character and ways to develop ourselves."

HIM "Like, what you'd do if you ever came face-to-face with a dragon?"

ME "Metaphorically, yes."

HIM "I have no dragons in my world."

ME "One day, you will."

HIM "How do you know?"

ME "Because we all fall in love, we all have our hearts broken, and we all, at some point, lose hope. There be dragons."

HIM "Then what's the fire-breathing?"

ME "I don't know. Lost metaphors?"

DIVORCE

One of my grade nine students has been out of sorts because of his parents' impending divorce. He decides to stay in the classroom with me during lunch.

ME "You know I got divorced, too?"

HIM "Really? You?"

ME "Yeah. A long time ago. Man, it hurt."

HIM "So, you have kids?"

ME "No. But I'll tell you this: if my wife and I had a kid like you, we would have prolonged our marriage for as long as we could, just like your parents did the past few years. I bet they stayed together this long just because of how much they love you."

HIM "They keep saying stuff like that."

ME "Because it's probably the truth."

HIM "It doesn't make me feel any better."

ME "No. It won't. But one day, it will."

LOL

I've just returned some marked essays, and one grade eleven student brings his up to my desk.

HIM "Sir, why did you circle this?"

ME "You wrote 'LOL' in your essay."

HIM "So? It's a word."

ME "Not really. It's an initialism. And it doesn't even make sense."

HIM "How? It's laughing ... *out loud*."

ME "All laughing is out loud."

HIM "I've seen people laugh quietly."

ME "That's called smiling."

IT'S ALL ABOUT THE ...

ME "What are your plans for the summer?"

GRADE TEN STUDENT "I don't know, sir. Chill with my boys. Play video games."

ME "You know when Benjamin Franklin was your age, he founded one of America's first independent newspapers?"

HIM "Who's that?"

ME "Benjamin Franklin? He was one of America's founding fathers."

He stares at me blankly.

ME "You ever see an American hundred-dollar bill?"

HIM "Is that why they call them Benjamins?"

ME "Enjoy your summer."

AGING

GRADE TEN STUDENT "Sir, how old are you?"

ME "Early forties."

HIM "Wow. You're older than my dad."

ME "Yup."

HIM "But you don't seem that old."

ME "Thanks, I guess."

HIM "Do you think about death a lot?"

ME "I'm thinking about it right now."

HIM "Why're you thinking about your death now?"

ME "I didn't say my death."

HIM "Oh."

CANADIAN, EH?

GRADE EIGHT STUDENT "Sir, did you know in Canada, we say 'eh,' and down in America, they say 'huh'?"

I whisper something.

HER "Sorry?"

I whisper again.

HER "Huh?"
ME "So, you're American now?"
HER "What?"
ME "Eh?"
HER "Sir!"

PRINCE

ENGLISH ELEVEN STUDENT "Sir, favourite guitarist?"
ME "Prince."
HIM "Really? Why him?"
ME "Have you ever tried to play lead guitar while dancing in platform heels?"
HIM "I don't usually look for those qualities in a guitarist."
ME "If you'd been around in the eighties, you would."

SOCCER

GRADE NINE STUDENT "Sir, why do we call it soccer instead of football like everyone else?"
ME "I'm not sure. Why don't you look it up for us?"
HER "Is it because we're copying American culture?"

ME "Good guess, but I have no clue. You should go on the computer there and find out."

HER "Maybe it's because—"

ME "You're going to keep guessing until I look it up for you, right?"

HER "That was the plan."

BLACKBOARD JUNGLE

I walk into my English 9 class and see that someone has written an inappropriate phrase on the board in huge letters. It involves a pun using my last name. The students are giggling.

ME "All right. I'm not even going to bother asking who did this. But I'll give extra credit to the first one who erases it."

A few students jump up, but one boy reaches the eraser first.

ME "Man, you've got some nerve. First you write it on the board, and now you try to take credit for cleaning it up?"

HIM "It was Derek! Not me."

ME "Thanks."

DEREK "Every time!"

A LIFE LESS MEATY

GRADE EIGHT STUDENT "Sir, why aren't you a vegetarian?"

ME "Probably because I like meat too much."

HER "You'd live longer."

ME "Yeah?"

HER "Yeah. It would suck if you died too soon."

ME "Good point."

HER "It would suck if we had to get another teacher."

ME "Yeah. Both those things would suck."

HER "We like you."

ME "Then I'll do my best not to die too soon."

HER "So you'll quit eating meat?"

ME "No."

ALWAYS KEEP IT SHORT

GRADE TEN STUDENT "Sir, what's up with your shorts?"

The students start laughing.

ME "What's wrong with these?"

HIM "They're, like, way too short."

ME "They're barely above my knees."

HIM "That's so old-school, sir."

ME "I don't know if you've noticed, but I'm kind of old-school."

STUDENT 2 "And you got those big pleats. Who wears pleats on their shorts anymore?"

His friends are beside themselves with laughter. I take it all in good-naturedly.

ME "All right, all right. Who else wants to have a go at my shorts?"

STUDENT 3 "Those are like *almost pants*."

STUDENT 1 (To Student 3) "That's what shorts are!"

The students lose it and are now laughing at Student 3.

ME "There's always one who flies too close to the sun."

BONUS QUESTION

I have handed out the *Macbeth* final exam for English 11. I have written a bonus question at the end: *For one point, ask yourself any question about Shakespeare. For two points, answer that question.*

A student raises his hand.

ME "Yes?"

HIM "What if I have a really good question for the bonus but don't know the answer?"

Giggling starts to spread throughout the room.

ME "Sorry, I'm not going to help you out on this one. You're on your own."

HIM "Okay."

Three minutes later.

HIM "Oh! Right!"

RINGS

GRADE TEN STUDENT "Sir, why don't you wear a wedding ring?"

ME "I'm not married."

HER "But you said you're in a common-law union with your girlfriend. It's like being married."

ME "I just don't like rings."

HER "Are you afraid it'll keep other women away?"

ME "Excuse me?"

HER "I know how men work. When the wife's away, it's time to play."

ME "Where do you get this stuff?"

HER "I read a lot of books."

HEAD INJURY

A grade nine student has a huge bruise on his forehead.

ME "What happened?"

His friends start giggling.

HIM "I hurt my head."
ME "I can see that. How?"
HIM "I ran into a locker yesterday."

I look deadpan around the room. The students are laughing.

ME "Okay, I'm going to ask: Why?"
HIM "I'm not sure. I thought it would be funny."
ME "Did you do it to impress the girls?"
HIM "No!"
ME "To impress your buddies?"
HIM "No!"

His friends challenge him on that.

HIM "Okay. Maybe they dared me."
ME (To his friends) "Were any of you impressed?"

They shake their heads no.

ME "I want you to remember this moment. Please know that for the rest of your life, you're now the guy in school who ran into a locker for no reason."
HIM "I don't think I can remember anything right now."

KEEPING MY MARBLES

I have brought a bag of marbles from home as part of a demonstration for my English 8 class.

STUDENT "Sir, why do you have those?"
ME "I'm going to show you something."
HIM "I mean, what do you use them for at home?"
ME "We used to play games with these when I was a kid."
HIM "How?"
ME "My friends and I would each bring our bags of marbles and roll them at each other, and if you won, you got to keep some of the other kid's marbles."
HIM "What was the game called?"
ME "Marbles."
HIM "Man, that's sad. Were all of your friends poor, too?"

SNACKS

GRADE TEN STUDENT "Sir, you have any snacks in the back room?"
ME "I have granola bars, power bars and cereal. You hungry?"
HIM "You have any chips?"
ME "No."
HIM "Why don't you have chips?"
ME "I try to stock up on healthier snack options. You should try to avoid chips."
HIM "Sir, I'm fifteen. I'll burn off any junk I put in my body. It's not like I'm your age."
ME "You have a weird way of asking for free food."

WAR AND PEACE

GRADE ELEVEN STUDENT "Sir, which novel have you read and thought was a total waste of time?"

ME "Tolstoy's *War and Peace*."

HIM "Really? That's a classic!"

ME "I know. It just didn't do it for me. It's subjective, like my curriculum. I know there's no way you'll love all of the books I choose for the class."

HIM "So I don't have to read them?"

ME "Nice try."

EMOTICONS

While handing back essays to my English 10 class ...

STUDENT "Sir, what's this?"

I walk over and see her pointing at something I've circled.

ME "That's a smiley face. You don't need to put a smiley face in your essay."

HER "I wanted you to know I was joking."

ME "If you write effectively, I'll know you're joking. You don't need to signal it with an emoticon."

HER "When you text your friends, how do they know you're joking?"

ME "I deliver the joke properly."

HER "That doesn't always work."

ME "Then they don't get it, or it was a bad joke."

HER "It's just *joking*, sir. You make it so difficult!"

FLY-FISHING

GRADE ELEVEN STUDENT "Sir, one of the other teachers told me you're a fly-fisherman."

ME "When I'm lucky, yeah. But usually I'm just a guy tossing a line in the water."

HIM "Why fly-fishing? Isn't spin casting easier?"

ME "It's not so much about catching fish for me. It's about being out on the water, catching on to nature's rhythms, forgetting everything for a few hours."

HIM "You're not married, are you?"

ME "No."

A THING FOR FEET

GRADE TEN STUDENT "Sir, you have nice feet."

I look down at my sandals.

ME "Thanks."

HER "You should be a foot model."

I laugh.

ME "Thanks. I'll take that as a compliment."

HER "Why wouldn't you?"

ME "Well, if someone comes up to you and says, 'You should be a *foot* model,' what's the implication?"

HER "You're lazy and never walk?"

ME "I'll take the compliment."

LED ZEPPELIN

GRADE ELEVEN STUDENT "Sir, I looked it up like you told me. You're right. 'The Battle of Evermore' is totally about *The Lord of the Rings.*"

ME "See? Pretty cool, eh?"

HIM "Yeah. It's just so trippy imagining him listening to Led Zeppelin."

ME "Who?"

HIM "Tolkien."

I laugh. He's not laughing.

ME "I have a bit more research for you to do."

NOT REALLY

GRADE ELEVEN STUDENT "Sir, it's so hot in here."

ME "It's summer. It's supposed to be hot."

HER "But it's hotter here than in my math class."

ME "We've got the southern exposure and no circulation. This is as good as it gets for us."

HER "You should ask for a different room."

ME "They're all in use."

HER "How about air conditioning?"

ME "You know there are kids in Africa attending classes in weather way hotter than this."

HER "You're like my dad—always comparing things to Africa."

POINT MISSED

GRADE TEN STUDENT "Sir, when did you realize you wanted to
be a teacher?"

ME "I had back surgery at a critical point in my life, which left
me with a lot of time to read and reflect. I realized I had two
loves: literature and helping young people find direction. Being
an English teacher seemed a good way to combine those two
passions."

HIM "All because you were stuck in bed after the hospital?"

ME "Yeah."

HIM "I can't wait to tell my mom that story next time she yells at me
for lying around in bed all day."

FINAL THOUGHTS

ME (To the class) "I know it's Friday, but if you could finish reading the chapter and then answer this essay question from the board over the weekend, that'd be great."

GRADE TWELVE STUDENT (Quietly) "You suck."

ME "Excuse me?"

HIM "Sorry. You suck, *sir.*"

In 1995, I became a certified high school English teacher in Vancouver, British Columbia. As every teacher will attest, nothing prepares you for that first year of teaching. I had seven preps (i.e., seven different courses for which I had to prepare seven different lessons and units) in five different classrooms. There were days when I thought I would burn out before the year was over. But a few months in, I remembered some advice my faculty associate gave me during my teaching practicum: keep a teaching journal to facilitate a reflective practice.

It was good advice. If I wanted to encourage young people to learn, I had to become a learner myself, with me as my subject area. So, whenever I had a chance, I would write in my journal, reflecting on the days that had passed and critiquing my own teaching style: things to improve, things that went well, ideas to pursue.

However, as with all journals, mine took on a life of its own as I began jotting down things my students said. They were often funny—sometimes on purpose. My Humanities 8 class was a limitless source of entertainment, as I would circulate among the groupings of desks during co-operative learning exercises, listening in on the ways they related to each other—or didn't. Every day, I would find myself trying my best not to crack up at something they said in earnest. And several times, I would rush to my desk to make a quick note of who said what to remind myself later of what happened that day. These journals would pile up over six more years of teaching.

Then, near the end of 1999, I found myself jotting down jokes that popped into my head. Quite often, these jokes would have nothing whatsoever to do with teaching. They were non sequiturs, written purely for my own amusement. These jokes would eventually form the backbone of my stand-up comedy act, which I would begin to pursue in February 2000.

In 2002, I found myself growing weary of teaching. I found the rigours of marking, the endless paperwork and our provincial government's refusal to properly fund public education were ever-growing thorns in my side. This was mainly because my other calling— comedy—was demanding more of my attention. And I learned that if you're not 100 percent invested in teaching, it will suck you dry, leaving you bereft of the energy and spirit required to enjoy life. You cannot fake teaching. So I quit.

I pursued stand-up comedy and did fairly well for a comedian who did not want to move to the United States. I toured; I wrote and performed, sporadically, for television and radio. I hosted a daily TV show called *The CityNews List* with some of my best friends in the business (one of them is the editor of this very book). It was a fun, exciting time.

Until 2010.

I had lost my TV show and found myself onstage every week going through the motions of comedy without feeling any of its joyous, reckless spirit.

It was time to reassess. I made a list of all the things that brought me joy in my life, as well as the ones that did not.

And that's when I realized: I missed teaching.

I missed the thrill of working with a reluctant learner and *hooking* them into a lesson or idea. I missed having a student come to me during the break to share the struggles going on in their life and ask me to just be there with them through it all. I missed seeing the glint in a young person's eye when they finally *get it*. And given my new experiences in the entertainment business, I knew I could better balance teaching and comedy this time around.

When I returned to teaching later that year, I continued writing in that journal and started a blog to share those stories with others. (This book contains some of the original entries from that blog, which ran from 2012 to 2015.) And I taught with new-found vigour, insight and wisdom, with more teaching tools in my belt—for four more years.

By 2015, my fiction podcast, *The Black Tapes*, had found an audience larger than I ever could have hoped for or imagined, and suddenly demanded my full-time attention. I now work in podcasting and TV development and split my time between Vancouver and Los Angeles, as far removed from the rigours of the classroom as could be.

But even in my new-found career I find myself using all the skills I learned and used in the classroom: listening, sharing and making myself vulnerable. Because as much as I like to think I've given to my students, they've given me so much more. I may have been their teacher in title, but more often than not, I found myself their student.

And they do not suck.

PHOTO: KAROLINA TUREK

Paul Bae is a comedian, writer, actor and podcaster. He is the award-winning co-creator and co-writer of the podcast *The Black Tapes* and the author and producer of the critically acclaimed podcast *The Big Loop*. He lives in Lions Bay, BC.